Travel with
Insider
Tips

www.marco-polo.com

Contents

For chapters: See inside front cover

TOP 10

Jot to be missed!

Jur TOP 10 hits – from the absolute No. 1 to No. 10 –
ielp you plan your tour of the most important sights.

UBUD ➤ 74

On the edge of the highlands, Ubud s nestled in an exotic landscape of ush rice terraces with the sacred olcano, Gunung Agung, looming bove it – this is the artistic and ultural heartland of the island.

PURA TANAH LOT ➤ 48

or many, this is the Bali experience ney will remember – the sea temple, urrounded by the waves of the ndian Ocean, with the setting sun n the background.

GUNUNG BATUR & DANAU BATUR ➤ 132

ake Batur forms part of one of he most spectacular volcanic andscapes on the planet, a huge caldera from which the eponymous olcano rises up (left).

PURA BESAKIH ➤ 104

Pura Besakih – which is made up of around 30 temple complexes with nore than 200 buildings – is considered the "mother" of all Bali temples and is the centre of religious life.

TIRTAGANGGA ➤ 109

f Oscars were awarded for cinematic views, the vista over the rice terraces to the distant sea and the neighbouring island of Lombok would be a very strong contender.

6 PURA LUHUR ULU WATU ➤ 50

The "temple over the rock" and the waves smashing against the coast 100m (330ft) down below are the two extremes of this unforgettable panorama.

7 DANAU BRATAN ➤ 137

When you see this mountain lake, embedded in the rainforest and surrounded by volcanoes, you will understand why the Danau Bratan is sacred to the Balinese.

8 BANGLI ➤ 80

The former royal village in the midst of verdant nature is home to one of the three most sacred temples on the island – it is hard to imagine a more magical location than this.

9 PULAU MENJANGAN ➤ 156

The pristine waters surrounding this nature reserve island offer crystal clear views of the marine world, even at a depth of 40m (130ft), making it the best dive spot in Bali.

10 KUTA ➤ 53

Sun, beach and fun – that is the dream for those who chose Kuta, possibly Southeast Asia's most vibrant package tourism destination.

THAT BALI

Experience Bali's unique flair and find out what makes it tick – just like the Balinese themselves.

A FESTIVAL FOR THE GODS

Temple festivals offer unforgettable insights into Balinese spirituality. Through meditation, prayers, mantras and rituals, the faithful invite the gods to visit the temple; gamelan music creates a magical atmosphere while special delicacies take care of physical wellbeing. The tourist information offices list the current temple festivities.

STAY WITH LOCALS

There is no better way to connect with the local population than by moving in with them on a so-called "homestay". This will give you the kind of insights into everyday Balinese life that most tourists will not encounter. Throughout the island, hundreds of host families run small residences – especially in the mountainous interior – where heartfelt Balinese hospitality is still a way of life. In the up-and-coming holiday village of Munduk (➤ 144), visitors can even help with the harvest. Bali Homestay (www.bali-homestay.com) and other organisations will help you to find homestay accommodation.

Yoga and meditation are inextricably interwoven with Hindu religion and Balinese culture

FEELING

ODY AND SOUL

ver since the Hollywood film *Eat ?ray Love* with Julia Roberts, legions f tourists – most of them women – ave followed the lead of the pro-agonist, Liz Gilbert, in her attempt o find herself and peace of mind n one of the many yoga, meditation nd healing centres in Ubud (➤ 74) nd other places on Bali.

TASTE THE FRUITS

Papayas, mangos and coconuts – you know all of these tropical fruits, not to mention bananas and pine-apples – but the truly tropical and exotic fruits rarely find their way into our supermarkets. On Bali you will be able to taste them all (cheaply) in the local markets. There are fruits with unusual names such as

rambutan, *longan* and *durian* and when you try them at the markets you will also get an idea of everyday Balinese life. The markets in Ubud (Jl. Raya Ubud; daily 6am–1pm), Sukawati (Jl. Raya Sukawati; daily 6am–8pm), Jimbaran (Jl. Ulu Watu; daily 6am–noon) and Denpasar (Pasar Badung, Jl. Gajah Mada; daily 6am–8pm) are especially attractive.

STREET FEAST

International dishes may have the advantage in that there are no surprises but these surprises are what make travel so interesting. No matter whether it is *Babi Guling* (suckling pig stuffed with spices), *Gado Gado* (warm vegetable salad with peanut sauce), *Nasi Campur* (rice with side dishes) or one of the many other Balinese specialities – the best way to explore the island's cuisine is to go to one of the ubiquitous *warungs*, food stalls with one table, two benches and an awning to provide protection from the sun.

BEACH LIFE

The beach is the stage for many holiday dreams and even if Bali does not have the most beautiful beaches on the planet, they still play a large part in most holiday visits. There are sandy beaches that stretch for miles, such as in Kuta (➤ 53) and Balian (➤ 161), as well as the smaller coves framed by cliffs on the Bukit Badung Peninsula (➤ 58) with their simple *warungs*.

VILLAGE LIFE

Most Balinese come from villages (➤ 16), so to understand their way of life you should head for the traditional village of Penglipuran (➤ 17). Here visitors can visit the homes of the residents, watch them carrying out their handiwork and even have a chat with them.

JOURNEY THROUGH TIME

Some places in our world have a charm and beauty that are incomparable. The small island of Gili Trawangan (➤ 173) is one of them, and this is where those in search of romantic island life can experience what Bali was like before the arrival of tourism.

Order a *rijsttafel* and enjoy a multitude of Indonesian specialties

The Magazine

Agama Hindu Dharma
FAITH and EVERYDAY LIFE

In the dualistic worldview of Agama Hindu Dharma, the unique religion of the Balinese, an antagonistic relationship exists between the macrocosm (the universe) and the microcosm (humans). Man lives in a cosmos of opposites such as heaven and earth, mountain and sea, life and death, and good and evil, and his existence is only possible through the interaction of these antipodes.

This syncretic religion unites elements of Hinduism, Buddhism, and ancient beliefs in the spirit world, in which everything is connected with everything else. This means that one force is only as good as the opposing one and this in turn means that a person's aim should be to satisfy the law of the world, *dharma*, that regulates harmony between opposites, through his actions that are known as his *karma*. This explains why the Balinese pay homage to the gods as well as the demons.

The faithful bathing in the holy spring waters of Pura Tirta Empul

And, as the pantheon of gods on Bali is so enormous, the everyday life of the Balinese is determined to a great extent by sacrificial rites and ceremonies.

Faith is Life and Life is Faith

On Bali, everything is faith and all aspects of life are permeated by religion. Even in the tourist centres, one has to take great care not to step on sacrificial offerings. Small baskets woven out of banana leaves with small rice and fruit pyramids are placed in front of the doors of homes, boutiques, restaurants and discotheques, bus stops and crossroads. Incense sticks are intended to ward off evil and attract good; nearly every rice field and bridge has a shrine; each family and farm has its own temple and each village has at least three (► 16). And so it is not surprising that Bali is known as the island of ten thousand temples.

Temporary Seats for Visiting Gods

Balinese temples (*pura*) are not grandiose buildings with ornate halls and towers, with statues of the gods glittering with gold beneath impressive arches. Rather, at first glance, they seem to be inconspicuous buildings that were not erected to provide the gods with a splendid house but as a means with which to contact them through specific rituals. They are always open places, surrounded by walls that protect against demons, and are divided into courtyards, aligned in the axes of mountain-sea (for good and evil), and east-west (for the rising and setting sun). In keeping with the cosmic order, they are organised as three zones and the layout follows a set scheme.

Offerings for the gods at the village temple in Blungbang

TEMPLE TOP 10

❶ **Pura Tanah Lot** (➤48): The sunset at Bali's most famous sea temple is possibly the island's most popular postcard motif.

❷ **Pura Besakih** (➤104): Bali's largest and holiest temple is worth visiting if only to experience its unique atmosphere.

❸ **Pura Luhur Ulu Watu** (➤50): Perched high above the sea, this temple has a spectacular location on a cliff.

❹ **Pura Luhur Batukau** (➤89): Surrounded by jungle and frequently shrouded in mist, this temple – which is only rarely visited by tourists – is perhaps the one with the most magical aura on Bali.

❺ **Pura Kehen** (➤80): The Pura Kehen mountain temple is one of Bali's most important temples and also one of its most beautiful.

❻ **Pura Taman Ayun** (➤86): Surrounded by a lotus pond and a stunning park, a visit to this temple is an absolute must on your trip to Bali.

❼ **Pura Ulun Danu Bratan** (➤137): Partially built on artificial islands in Lake Bratan, and surrounded by a verdant park, this temple is dedicated to the rice goddess and exudes a mystical charm, especially in the early morning hours.

❽ **Pura Ulun Danu Batur** (➤132): This is a temple of superlatives, not least because of its location on Lake Batur and its views of the volcano.

❾ **Brahma Vihara Arama** (➤145): Buddha statues and buildings shining in gold characterise the island's only Buddhist monastery complex.

❿ **Pura Meduwe Karang** (➤127) The extraordinary reliefs and statues make this temple in Kubutambahan unique on the island.

Temple Prototype

The entrance is always through a single door aligned with the sea and the *candi bentar*, a split gate that is open above and intended to give expression to the complementary forces of the cosmos. Beyond this is the first temple courtyard, the *jaba sisi*, representing the earthly world, with several pavilions where the faithful (*bale*) can rest and a cockfighting arena (*wantilan*), which also serves as a preparation site for dances, festivities and rituals.

Next is the *jaba tengah* (middle courtyard) a large, open assembly hall (*bale agung*) dominated by a big signal drum (*kulkul*), which is beaten to summon the faithful to the temple. The *kori agung*, a richly ornamented gate decorated with stonework that is closed at the top, is flanked by two powerful guardian figures (*raksasa*) and symbolises the transition of man from one existence into the other and, in doing so, the belief in reincarnation. It leads – after the *aling aling*, the wall protecting against demons – to the third and highest temple courtyard, and the *jeroan*.

This sanctuary, which is not accessible to tourists, serves as a dwelling place for the gods during their stay on earth. These *merus* are composed of stone bases that represent the foundation on which the world rests followed by a pagoda style structure, with a number of tiered roofs covered with palm leaves, showing the rank of the deity in the Balinese pantheon (the highest number – eleven – is for Shiva).

Island of SMILES and FAUX PAS

\ll personal relations on Bali are shaped by a willingness to ake into consideration the feelings of others. This makes it ıecessary to try to avoid any of the innumerable faux pas that :an easily trip up foreigner tourists.

'he Western world's cliché of Bali is usually that of a romantic tropical ›aradise where everyone is happy and smiling. The Balinese actually do .mile a lot, but this also serves as a protection mechanism to shield hem from social conflict. It conceals emotions and helps to overcome ıncertainty or embarrassment. The Balinese have many reasons to smile ›ut – in contrast to Western habits – they never at laugh anything, let lone another person.

;ocial Harmony

f a Balinese smiles when he is asked the way but does not give an ınswer, it is probably because he does not understand English. In order ıot to lose face, he will try to find somebody who can answer the question.

ven market haggling is done with a smile

A smile will help make your time in Bali all the more enjoyable

If that does not work, he will point in one direction or other so as to retain some shred of dignity. In a nutshell, allowing the other person to save face without losing one's own, is the important guiding principle in the rules of social conduct. That is why anyone who behaves aggressively, has emotional outbursts or speaks too loudly, is seen as destroying social harmony and damaging their reputation.

Hands and Feet

In some cases, you can really put your foot in it – with your hands – the left hand is considered impure and should never be used for eating or for handing over a present or an item. Putting hands pockets, on the hips or folding ones arms are all taken as signs of aggression. You should also never point your finger at another person. And, throwing something at somebody is also considered offensive – you only do that to animals.

Balinese never put their feet on the table, never cross their legs or sit on the floor with legs stretched out pointing towards someone. The head, on the other hand, is regarded as the seat of the mind and soul and is considered sacred by the Balinese. Touching it is an offense and that is why it is also taboo to pat a child on the head.

Other Stumbling Blocks

Direct criticism – especially if a third person is present – is considered to be a mild form of violence and displays of affection in public are also frowned upon. Especially in the countryside, it is considered unseemly for women to wear short skirts, skimpy T-shirts or tank tops, transparent blouses and other revealing clothing. Regardless of gender, it is considered vulgar to wear tight trousers and very short pants; even dirty or torn clothing is taken as a sign of disrespect.

'he Balinese prefer modest beachwear that covers the knees and shoulders

Timekeeping in Bali is something flexible, not something intended to)e actually binding but rather an indication. Coming to an appointment)n time is not an offense but is not the done thing to arrive punctually – 'ou should arrive about half an hour late. It is an absolute must to take)ff your footwear before entering a house; the greeting takes the form of ı light handshake (not a grip) with the right hand that is then placed on he chest. And, last but not least, always leave something small on your)late after you have finished eating. Follow these guidelines and you'll nanage to escape any social awkwardness.

TEMPLE ETIQUETTE

- It seems that tourists generally tend to behave like bulls in a china shop at temple festivities as they jostle and fight to get the best picture. They often push their way to the front, climb onto walls, run around between the worshipers, hold their cameras too close to the faces of those praying, use the flash – all these behaviours show disrespect and are inexcusable.
- Tourists who arrive at a temple in their beachwear, or in skimpy or dirty clothing, will not be allowed to enter the temple area. The same applies to those who try to go into the complex without a *selendang* (a temple sash). The sash is tied around one's hips and can usually be hired. However, the prices charged are often exorbitant so it is a good idea to buy an inexpensive sash soon after you arrive. It also makes sense to buy a sarong since they are mandatory for all men and women attending temple celebrations.
- In Balinese culture, blood is regarded as impure and it is therefore forbidden to visit a temple with open wounds or during menstruation.

Balinese Village MIRROR of the COSMOS

In Bali, the village community ranks immediately after one's own family. And, just as everything else on the island is determined by faith, the layout of the traditional Balinese village is also defined by the cosmic system.

As with all the temples on Bali (➤ 11), the villages on the island also reflect a miniature version of the Balinese macrocosm. To achieve this, they are surrounded by a wall to protect them from demons, laid out along an imaginary mountain-sea or east-west axis and divided into three sections that symbolise man's life cycle from birth to death.

Three Spheres

At the upper end of the village's main street, which runs between the two cardinal points of mountain and sea, is the *pura puseh* (temple of origin).

COCKFIGHTS

Some consider cockfighting as an ancient ritual, while others consider it an act of animal cruelty. Cockfights have been held on Bali for around 1,000 years and derive from religious traditions – the name *tabu rah* (meaning "spilled blood") implies a sacrifice to the gods. However, nowadays it is mostly a sport that involves lots of money with bets of 5 million rupiahs not being unusual. To make sure that the cocks put up a good long fight, they are pumped full of drugs, this makes the battle between the cocks even more grisly. There is only one survivor as the loser is always killed.

Village men prior to a cockfight (left); the main street in Penglipuran, a traditional Balinese village (centre); the *banjar* is a community meeting attended only by married men (right)

This temple always lies beyond the last homestead and is dedicated to the village founder and the ancestors. The ancestors are regarded as deities, since their legacy is the property of the village itself. The lower village, with the temple of the dead and cremation site, is located at the opposite end.

Between these two points is the centre of the village, which is always a square with a banyan tree towering over it. This is where you will find the main village temple, the music pavilion, the cockfighting arena and market, as well as the *banjar* assembly hall.

For the Common Good

The smallest social unit of Balinese society is the *banjar* village council, which dates back to the pre-Hindu era. Membership in the *banjar*, and participation in meetings, is obligatory for all families as this is where community issues are discussed, ceremonies and temple festivities organised, marriages arranged and divorces settled, new buildings planned, crops managed and many other affairs resolved. Crimes are sentenced according to the extremely complicated (but not codified) *adat* common law, which also dates to the pre-Hindu era. This law determines the behaviour, rights and responsibilities of the families. In addition, it also precisely defines how the village community is designed, so that individuals are able to live in harmony with the village, with themselves, their family, nature and the non-material world. This makes each village akin to a small state within the state, where social status is not determined by what a member possesses but by the extent to which they are committed to the common good and the benefit of all. The Balinese also know that many things do not function well above a certain size, so as soon as there are more than 500 villagers, a new *banjar* is established. This means that every city becomes a village, even ones as large as Kuta and Denpasar.

LIFE as a CELEBRATION

In Bali religious festivities divide the year into cycles, periods and rhythms, and are interwoven into everyday life. They are celebrated with great exuberance, are very colourful and the entire island takes part.

There are a considerable number of occasions and celebrations with over 200 official Balinese festivities. This is even more impressive given that Bali's festivities are determined by the Pawukon calendar, which only has 210 days in a year.

Temple Anniversary

This is exacerbated by the fact that each temple on Bali celebrates its anniversary once in the 210-day year. The Odalan festival is held on the anniversary of the consecration of each temple and the entire structure is then decorated with umbrellas and long, colourful ribbons and with flowers. Fruit is arranged into enormous pyramids and carried into the temple on the heads of the elaborately dressed women. In the temple the priests bless the offerings so that the gods can enjoy their spiritual essence and the faithful can eat the offerings afterwards. However, before this can happen, the deities are invoked to enter into the sacred images, which are carried in a solemn procession to the beach, or the closest lake or river, where they are ritually bathed. The exuberant part of the feast begins at night when palm wine flows like water, everyone jokes and laughs and there is music, dancing and games.

A Day of Silence

There is one day in the year when you do not want to arrive/depart or do anything at all in Bali: the Balinese New Year's Festival of Nyepi. It follows the lunar calendar and begins on a new moon night in March with processions letting off loud firecrackers. Incredibly loud music, shouting, gongs and drums, rattling and banging is all used to scare evil spirits and demons from the island. However, the spirits are very crafty and there is always

Left: Colourful monster figures are paraded through the streets on the day before Nyepi
Above: Towers of fruit offerings for the procession

the risk that – in spite of all the pandemonium – evil can be hiding away somewhere on the island and as a precaution against this, Bali is enveloped in complete darkness and silence from 6am on the following day. This is so that any lingering spirits and demons will be fooled into thinking that there is no life left on the island. It is forbidden for anyone to be on the streets, to go work, to set a fire, to turn on lights, play music and all cars, motorcycles and mopeds have to remain where they are. And, nobody is allowed to leave the house. It is not until 6am on the next day that the Balinese once again go about their everyday life.

INSIDER INFO

- There are around 20,000 temples on Bali and an average of 90 temple festivals every day. Even if you only stay on the island for a short time, you will have an excellent chance of being able to experience one of these festivals.
- The exact information on almost all of the festivals on Bali can be found in the annual *Bali Events Calendar* available from the tourist offices and online at www.bali-indonesia.com/events-calendar.htm.
- The Nyepi rule of silence also applies to foreign tourists, although the regulations are not quite as strict, if you leave the hotel or resort, you will certainly soon come across a village policeman (*pecalang*) who will order you back to where you came from. It is not possible to check in or out anywhere, all restaurants are closed and there is no public transport or taxis. It is good advice to stock up on all you need for a "retreat" day before it starts. The dates of the next Nyepi are 17 March 2018 and 7 March 2019.

Rice Terraces
STAIRS TO HEAVEN & HERITAGE SITE

Its peaceful atmosphere is what makes Bali so unique and this is especially true of the island's rural interior, where undulating rice terraces cover the steep mountain slopes in a series of green cascades, and the water in the flooded paddies gleams in the sunlight.

Over the course of millennium, the Balinese have laboured with nothing but hoes and shovels to built their remarkable rice terraces. So they definitely deserve their place on the UNESCO World Heritage List, which was officially granted in 2012. The best places to view the beautiful, tumbling terraces are near Tegallalang (➤ 77), Jati Luwih (➤ 89), Tista (➤ 172) and Tirtagangga (➤ 109).

Cooperative Agriculture

The Balinese call this landscape the "steps of the gods" or "stairs to heaven" and while they look like a unique work of art, they were actually created out of necessity. The island's topography meant that there was only a small amount of useable land available. This meant that that – even in the early days of settlement – there was insufficient grain to meet the population's needs. There was no alternative but to increase cultivation areas

Most rice in Bali is still cultivated using traditional methods

MANY NAMES, MANY MORE DUCKS

- On Bali, rice is not simply "rice", in the fields it is called *padi*, threshed rice is *gabah*, husked raw rice is *beras* and cooked rice is *nasi*.
- Balinese ducks live in the lap of luxury (at least, until they are slaughtered) and they form an essential part of rice production. They control insects and weeds in the fields and their droppings make the use of artificial fertilizers unnecessary.

through terracing. Since individuals couldn't undertake such a mammoth task, the *subak* was formed. This is a crop and irrigation cooperative tasked with organising the cultivation and harvesting of the rice, which dates back to the island's distant past. And the equitable distribution of water – 3,000–5,000 litres/8,00–1,300 gallons of flowing water are necessary to produce one kilo of rice – was done via a sophisticated system of canals and basins leading from the mountains to the terraces. Each rice farmer is a member of a *subak*, which also determines when, where and by whom the fields can be laid out, when planting, irrigation and harvesting is to take place, and how the yield is to be distributed.

Gift of the Gods

The *subak* also determines the frequency and dates of the sacrificial rites. Rice is not only the most important food on Bali (and in all of Asia) but is also venerated as a "gift of the gods" that is personified by Dewi Sri, the goddess of rice. She is the wife of Vishnu and offerings in the form of holy water, food and fragrant essences are made to her every day. In order not to avoid angering her, it is forbidden to say anything bad when working in the fields. Only if the goddess is completely content will she become "pregnant" (rice blossoming) and finally three to five months later, depending on the region and soil, she will "give birth" to grain after grain (the rice harvest).

Rice fields cover 25 per cent of the island, yielding up to three crops per year

On the Rim of the Ring of Fire

Shortly after 6am the sun appears between the Agung and Batur volcanoes and transforms the horizon with a dazzling play of colour. A little later, the two impressive cones stand out in silhouette against the light of the new day. It is no wonder that the volcanoes are sacred to the Balinese.

This is especially true of the 3,142m (10,308ft) Gunung Agung (➤ 106) the spiritual centre of Bali. According to Hindu-Balinese beliefs, the sacred mountain symbolises Meru, the centre of the universe, the seat of the Hindu trinity and all of the other deities, as well as the home of the spirits of deceased ancestors. And that is why the holiest temple on the island – the mother temple Pura Besakih (➤ 106) – is located on its slopes. The Pura Besakih is the axis of the Balinese system of coordinates; all temples, villages and houses are laid out in line with it, and people make sure their heads are pointed towards it when they go to sleep.

Unpredictable Sacred Mountain

The massive cone of this active stratovolcano can be seen from almost everywhere in Bali. It dominants the entire island of Bali along with the smaller Gunung Batur (1,717m/5,633ft; ➤ 132), Gunung Abang (2,153m/7,063ft), Gunung Batukaru (2,276m/7,467ft) and many other volcanoes that cover more than three quarters of the island.

Gunung Agung last displayed its divine power in March 1963 when it erupted, after lying dormant for 120 years, and devastated large parts of the eastern half of the island. Many villages were destroyed and thousands of people perished in the glowing streams of molten lava. Neighbouring Gunung Batur has still not quietened down; the last major eruptions occurred in 1917 and 1926, and it fired a warning shot in 1994 and light quakes were measured as recently as September 2009.

Tectonic Plates

On the neighbouring island of Java there are 35 volcanoes that are considered to be particularly dangerous. There are more than 125 active volcanoes in Indonesia and more than 200 eruptions have been registered since the start of record keeping, and there are up to 1,000 earthquakes every year. This high seismic activity is due to Indonesia's position on the edge of the almost 40,000km (25,000mi) Pacific Ring of Fire. In Bali's

Rice fields at the foot of Gunung Agung

case, the Sahul Plate, part of the Australian Plate, migrates at a rate of 6cm (2.4in) per year under the Sunda Plate (a section of the Eurasian Plate) every year. This creates cracks in the earth's crust and magma makes it way upwards through them, and earthquakes occur if the plates shift abruptly.

Creator and Destroyer

Despite the fact that volcano eruptions destroy all human activity, people have always preferred to settle on their slopes. Their destructive force yields extremely fertile volcanic soil and the fields on Bali, and the neighbouring islands, are among the most productive on earth. There are two to three rice crops every year – and this means that not only the landscape, but also the social development of the island has, to a large extent, been determined by volcanic activity. It has enabled the island's high population density – there are around 750 inhabitants per square kilometre – and stimulated the development of Bali's advanced culture.

Volcanoes are both destroyers and creators and, according to Hindu-Balinese beliefs, Bali was once flat and barren until the Hindu god Shiva – the source of creation and destruction – moved Meru (the centre of the universe) from India to Bali and split it into two parts: Agung and Batur.

THE ROOF OF BALI

For keen hikers and fit tourists, the greatest nature highlight on Bali is to stand on the summit of Gunung Agung or Gunung Batur at dawn, and watch as the rising sun casts its light on one of the world's most spectacular volcanic landscapes. The Batur is the less strenuous option (➤ 166, 169).

Gamelan
Pure as Moonlight

Bali really is the perfect destination for music lovers. Music plays a major role in daily life on the island and is as important as flowers, incense and offerings, prayer and meditation in temple and village ceremonies.

The air in Bali is always filled with the sound of music. No night passes without the valleys and hills resonating with the gentle tones of the large bronze gongs, cymbals and xylophones; no day without the streets reverberating to the sound of drums and percussions as the men and women bear their towers of fruit for the gods to the temple in solemn processions.

Magical Tones

On Bali – and also Java and Lombok to a certain extent – everything revolves around the gamelan. Religious celebrations, social events such as weddings and births, as well as dance dramas and shadow puppet plays are all accompanied by the appropriate music. This musical tradition can be traced back to pre-Hindu days and the Dutch ethnomusicologist Jaap Kunst once said that gamelan is "as pure and mysterious as moonlight and changes as often as flowing water".

However, it is sometimes difficult for Western ears to appreciate gamelan as the style of music is has major differences in melody, harmony, tuning

EXPERIENCE GAMELAN

Those interested in learning more about Balinese music can do so at the **Mekar Bhuana Conservatory** (Jl. Gandapura Gandapura III, no. 501X, Denpasar; tel: 0361 46 42 01; www.balimusicanddance.com). The island's main cultural institute has dozens of instruments and countless CDs and DVDs. Top quality gamelan lessons and dance classes are also available. Another address for gamelan instruction, and many other activities, is the **Pondok Pekak Library & Learning Center** (Monkey Forest Road, Ubud; tel: 0361 97 61 94; www.pondokpekaklibrary.com).

ınd scales. The gamelan sounds are based on the completely foreign ntervals of two different scales: the Chinese pentatonic scale and a ıeptatonic system.

t Began with a Mallet

Gamelan is mainly played with percussion instruments (*gamel* means "strike" or "mallet"). The most revered gamelan instrument is the large gong, which can have a diameter of up to 1m (3.3ft), and is used to punctuate the musical phrases. The metallophones are equipped with bamboo resonators and create the melodic elements while the cylindrical drums, which are covered with animal skin, assign the tempo, determine the beginning and end of the "melody" and the form of the composition.

This means that the drummer is the leader of the orchestra, which can consist of about ten to 40 musicians and twice as many instruments. Depending on the occasion, more than one orchestra can perform simultaneously and it is a very special experience to hear the various ones and tempos mix with different keynotes. When the Prince of Ubud died it is believed that almost 150 ensembles performed at the same time during the funeral celebrations. So it comes as no surprise that, with more than 6,000 gamelan orchestras, Bali is considered a traditional stronghold of this kind of music, which is also very popular on Java. Gamelan music has the lion's share of airtime on the radio and is also frequently heard in Thailand, Malaysia and the Philippines – albeit, in a slightly different form.

Percussion instruments are the defining element of gamelan, which is played by all sections of Bali's population

Milestones in History

There are no records of Bali's earliest history but, as 500,000-year-old early human fossils were found on the neighbouring island of Java, it is assumed that Bali was also settled early. The first people migrated from the Malayan Peninsula sometime around 2,500 BC.

They brought with them a highly developed culture and soon drove the indigenous population into the remote regions in the interior of the island. A cultural revolution took place in the Iron Age, which began in all probability with the immigration of Indians. They also established the first trading places on the archipelago from the 1st century AD.

The monument in Denpasar that commemorates the 1906 *puputan*

Inspired by India, Oppressed by the Netherlands

This led to the establishment of the first Hindu kingdom on Java, which started to spread to Bali in the 10th century. This empire collapsed the early 16th century with the advance of Islam; the Java elite fled to Bali, which then became the last bastion of Hinduism and soon split into several individual kingdoms.

VIEW HISTORY

- The bronze Puputan Memorial, on Tanah Lapang Puputan (➤ 60) central square in Denpasar, is dedicated to the mass ritual suicide of the royal court of Bandung. The figures emerge out of a stylised lotus blossom and sculptures express the true heroism of those who sacrifice themselves in this rite.
- Only a few metres away from this monument, you can immerse yourself in the island's history at the Bali Museum (➤ 60) with its exhibition of archaeological finds and other historical exhibits.

In the middle of the 19th century, Dutch colonial control expanded into Bali. Starting in the north, the Dutch conquered the entire island after years of fierce warfare. Only the ruler of Bandung – today's Denpasar – refused to bow to foreign rule although he had no chance of defeating it using military force. Along with his royal household, he decided on a mass ritual suicide and 2,000–4,000 Balinese died in the *puputan* in 1906. Another *puputan* took place in Klungkung in 1908 but Bali was not completely controlled by the Dutch until 1913. The Japanese invaders drove them out in 1942. After Japan's surrender, Indonesia declared its independence on 17 August 1945; however the Netherlands attempted to take over the country by force once again in 1947/48.

Out of the Frying Pan and into the Fire

In 1949 the Netherlands was forced to recognise the Republic of Indonesia, which was governed from Java at that time. Sukarno was named president and he attempted – in vain – to unite the nationalists, Communists and Muslim fundamentalists under the concept of a "managed democracy". The Communists initiated an uprising in the autumn of 1965 but tens of thousands perished on Bali alone during the right-wing counter-coup. Sukarno resigned in 1967 and General Suharto became the new head of state. He was one of the initiators of the massacre and soon called for the start of a "new order".

Suharto established a dictatorship and made himself the centre of a cult of personality

Between Dictatorship and Democracy

However, this term was just a cover for a reign of terror and violence. The archipelago was now under dictatorial rule; any form of opposition was immediately suppressed and religious freedom gradually eroded in favour of Islam. The anger of the people finally exploded after three decades, leading to Suharto's resignation in 1998, which was followed by the first democratic presidential election. This ultimately led to more peaceful times although they too were marred by the Islamist bombings that shattered Bali in 2002 and 2005. More than 220 people in the Hindu enclave in the world's largest Muslim nation perished in the attacks. Today Indonesia seems to have consolidated its democracy; the terrorist activities of the years around the turn of the millennium are in the past and tourism on Bali is growing every year.

Bali Dances

The Balinese have dance performance to fit every ceremony, celebration and occasion. More than different 200 dances are known on the island and, no matter how small, each village has its own dance group. Dancing can be the simple expression of the joy of being alive or it can have a profound religious significance but either way the performances are almost always of exceptionally high standards.

Balinese dances have long become part of the standard repertoire for entertaining tourists but the dance dramas that are performed on dozens of stages in the tourist resorts are also a wonderful example of how traditions, dating back thousands of years, and tourist marketing, can enjoy a profitable coexistence. Especially in Ubud, the dances – which are always accompanied by a gamelan orchestra (➤ 25) – are as much a part of everyday life as rice is a part every Balinese meal. When you watch the spectacularly colourful performances for the first time you will find that your camera's memory card will soon be full. Two of the most popular dances, which are performed regularly in the tourist centres, are the Barong and Legong.

Good Versus Evil

The Barong, which has its origins in pre-Hindu days, is particularly dramatic. The seven acts symbolise the eternal struggle between good and evil. The mythical lion-like creature Barong, the protector of mankind, personifies good while the terrifying witch Ragda personifies evil. The highlight of the event occurs when Barong summons his helpers – men

BALINESE DANCE DRAMA

The best place to experience the magical world of Balinese dance dramas is in Ubud, where numerous performances are held every evening (➤ 75). Batubulan is not far away and is another centre of Balinese dance. Here, performances are usually held every morning at 9am in front of a magnificent temple, making it ideal for photographers (➤ 83). The Legong, in particular, is often performed free of charge as you enjoy your restaurant dinner but although these performances are often of a high quality, the ambience is frequently not that appropriate.

DANCE CLASSES

Dance workshops offer the opportunity learn more about Balinese dance – they are held in the **Pondok Pekak Library & Learning Center** (➤ 25) and the **Mekar Bhuana Conservatory** in Denpasar (➤ 25) and at other locations.

armed with the *kris*, a dagger with magical powers. However, Ragda uses her witchcraft to put the warriors in a trance that makes them turn their daggers on themselves. Barong is able to break the spell and the dancers awaken slowly – unharmed. And so, the battle ends – as it must in a Balinese version – in a draw. Good and evil, the antagonistic forces of the cosmos remain inextricably linked together in order to keep the world in balance.

Dance of the Divine Nymphs

In stark contrast to the almost hypnotic Barong, is the extremely graceful and charming Legong. It is a kind of classical Balinese ballet and was first performed at the courts on Bali in the 19th century. Two or three girls in elaborate brocade robes appear as the embodiment of divine nymphs; they dance in a mirror image of carefully calculated steps and then separate into the individual characters to portray a legend from the 13th century in pantomime form. A pamphlet explains to foreign visitors that the performance is the story of a king's unrequited love for a princess. Each pose, each movement and each eyelid movement are determined with great precision and painstakingly rehearsed. As the Legong must be pure, girls who have not reached puberty are the only ones who are allowed to perform the dance it. After years of training they make their first appearance at eight to ten years of age.

The Legong (previous page) is charming and graceful while the Barong is more martial and colourful

Finding Your Feet

First Two Hours

The majority of tourists arrive in Bali by plane. However, those who are on a trip through Indonesia or Southeast Asia can also travel by train (Java) and ferry.

Passport and Visas

- Your **passport** must be valid for at least six months after your date of arrival in Indonesia and **children** under 16 need their own passport.
- Citizens of certain countries, including Britain, Ireland, Australia, New Zealand, Canada and the US, can enter **without a visa** if the visit is purely for tourism and the stay is not longer than 30 days. You must have a valid **return or onward ticket** when you enter and exit one of Indonesia's international airports (including Denpasar).
- Persons not travelling to Indonesia purely for tourism purposes, or those wanting to stay in the country for longer than 30 days, will need a **visa**. The visa is stamped into your passport on entry; it is initially valid for 30 days and costs US$35, which must be paid in cash in one of the accepted major currencies. A return ticket must also be presented.
- The visa can only be **extended once** by 30 days. The application must be made seven days prior to your expiry date at an Imigrasi office, the Indonesian immigration services (in Kuta, Denpasar and Singaraja) and costs US$30. You passport will be retained (copy required) while your visa extension is being processed.

Arriving by Air

- There are direct **international flights** to Bali from Australia and Asia but there are no direct flights from Europe or North America. Arriving from those areas will mean connections on the Arabian Peninsula or with other Southeast Asian airports.
- Bali is a popular package tour destination so it is a good idea to check the internet for special deals through **booking websites** such as Expedia (www.expedia.com), Opodo (www.opodo.com) and Bookings.com (www.bookings.com) to see what they offer.
- The flight time from Europe to Bali is around 16–18 hours. However, you will have to make a **stopover** on the ca. 13,500km (8,400mi) direct distance; this depends on the airline but is usually on the Arabian Peninsula or in Bangkok, Kuala Lumpur, Singapore or Jakarta.

Ngurah Rai International Airport

- All national and international flights land at Ngurah Rai International Airport, **13km (8mi) south of Denpasar, the island's capital**, which is close to the major holiday centres in the south of Bali.
- Although it was recently renovated and expanded, **Ngurah Rai International Airport** (DPS; tel: 0361 9 35 10 11; www.baliairport.com) still struggles to handle the volume of tourists so it can take quite some time to clear through customs.
- Once you have taken care of the entry formalities and collected your luggage, you should withdraw some money. There are several **cash dispensers (ATMs)** and the exchange rates are much better than at the airport bureau de change.

Insider Tip

- The major international **car rental companies** are in the arrivals terminal and that is where you will also find an accommodation service, if you haven't already reserved your room. If you have arranged for an airport transfer, this is where you will be collected.
- Outside of the arrival hall on the right, you will find the **Koperasi Taxi Service** counter where you pay upfront for your destination: to Kuta Rp50,000, Legian Rp55,000, Seminyak Rp60,000, Jimbaran Rp75,000, Sanur Rp95,000, Nusa Dua Rp110,000, Ubud Rp195,000 and to Candi Dasa Rp335,000.
- If you want to go to Sanur, Nusa Dua, Ubud or Candi Dasa from the airport, you must ask to go via the **Bali Mandara Toll Road**, a causeway bridge across Benoa Bay that was opened in 2013. This route saves a lot of time and is also quite impressive and the additional – ridiculously cheap – toll of Rp10,000 is money well spent.

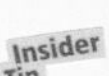

Arriving by Train and Ferry

- Travellers who are already in Indonesia can make the trip from Java to Bali by train and ferry – but this is far more **time-consuming**.
- There are regular train services from Jakarta and Yogyakarta to the ferry harbour at **Ketapang** (not far to the north of Banyunwangi) at the eastern end of Java (travelling time ca. 16 hours). There, you will have to transfer onto the car ferry to **Gilimanuk,** on the western tip of Bali. There are frequent crossings throughout the day and the trip takes ca. 30–45 minutes.
- There are no railways on Bali and you will have to continue your journey by bus (➤ 35).

Getting Around

When you feel like you've spent too much time at the beach or the pool, and boredom sets in, then it's time to set out on an island excursion. The only question is – where to?

Car Rental

- Exploring Bali in a rental car or motorcycle might not be the most sustainable and sociable way of travelling, but it is definitely the one that will give you the **most freedom**. Compared with many other countries, renting a vehicle in Bali is a real bargain and an increasing number of tourists decide to use a car for the entire duration of their stay.
- An **international driver's licence** is required for both a car and moped. The rental companies in Bali do not always take this requirement seriously but the police do (if you do not have one, there is an unofficial fine of Rp100, 000 instead of the official one that is close to Rp2 million). The **minimum age** limit is 21 but this is also rarely enforced.
- There is an oversupply of rental cars, which means that the **prices** are extremely low. Experience has shown that they are especially reasonable where competition is greatest and that means in the holiday centres in the south of Bali, particularly in Kuta and Sanur. There, you can hire a small car for as little as Rp150,000 per day,

a mid-sized sedan from Rp290,000, SUVs from Rp365,000 and a minibus for six or more people from Rp350,000–440,000 while the open-top version of the popular Suzuki jeeps costs around Rp290,000 per day. The prices include **unlimited mileage** and **comprehensive insurance** coverage (but be sure to check the policy).

- It goes without saying that you should check the vehicle's **roadworthiness** when you **collect** (pay special attention to the brakes, tyres and lights) and also check for any damage. In addition, make sure to receive a rental contract and the vehicle documents.
- People who do not want to deal with the clogged – and chaotic – traffic on Bali can **rent a car with driver**; this costs around Rp100,000 a day. It is easy to find a driver, you can either ask at the car rental office or approach the people who walk around on the streets offering transport. If you want to save yourself from being frustrated later, you should make it clear from the start that you do not want to be driven to the standard tourist traps. You pay the costs for the driver's meals while you are en route (ca. Rp20,000 per meal) and – of course – if there are any overnight stays, you will also have to cover his costs.
- Rental **mopeds** are the most popular means of transport for tourists on Bali. However, the number of moped accidents every year involving foreigners runs into the thousands. You should therefore only rent a moped if you really know how to handle it – and if you are fearless. Most of the mopeds available are semi- or fully-automatic models with a cylinder capacity of 125cc (7.6cu in) and the prices range from Rp44,000–60,000 per day with lower rates for rentals of a week or longer. Off-road motorcycles (125cc/7.6 cu in) and road bikes (150cc/9.1cu in) are also available and cost ca. Rp175,000. It is **compulsory** to wear a **helmet** and be **insured**.
- Car and moped hire companies are a dime a dozen in Bali so it is not necessary make a reservation in advance or to book a package deal that includes a vehicle – even in high season. In most cases, the international companies are considerably more expensive than their local competitors – and the offer is identical.
- Driving in Bali is on the left side of the road so that may take some getting used to if that is not the standard in your home country. But you will find it even more difficult to come to grips with the local's disregard for **traffic rules**. Indonesian drivers tend to be very creative about adhering to traffic regulations. You can expect to see oncoming traffic in a one-way street, red traffic lights being ignored, cars travelling without lights at night (or with high beams) and vehicles turning right while their indicators blink left.
- **Other dangers** include animals and children playing in the road and potholes in all sizes on the roads. You need to be a particularly cautious driver to meet the challenges posed by all of these risks. Drive slowly and do as the Balinese do when overtaking other cars or pedestrians – always blow your horn and also flash your headlights at night.
- **Petrol** (in Indonesian "premium") currently costs around Rp7,500 per litre, diesel (Solar) about Rp6,300. However, you will only be charged these prices at the official filling stations, which are generally restricted to the main roads. Off the beaten track, fuel is pumped into the tank from 400 litre barrels (88gal) or out of plastic bottles and costs around 50% more than at the petrol stations.

- There is no **towing/breakdown service** on Bali; if you have any mechanical problems, you must contact the rental company. This is also the case if you have an accident – and the police must always be notified.

Tourist Shuttle Buses

- Tour buses are not common on Bali but there are several companies that operate tourist shuttle buses in the resorts. The largest and most reliable is **Perama** (main office in Kuta, Jl. Legian 39; tel: 0361 75 18 75 and 0361 75 08 08; www.peramatour.com). The company operates modern air-conditioned buses and also offers transfers to and from your accommodation.
- The **prices** are reasonable, with a trip from Kuta to Lovina costing around Rp125,000, to Padang Bai Rp75,000 and to Ubud Rp60,000.
- Perama also operates boats and the company offers bus/boat transfers from all the holiday resorts on Bali to Gili Trawangan/Lombok, as well as to Nusa Penida and Nusa Lembongan. Bookings can be made online and you can also use private transfers.

Taxis

- There are no lack of taxis in the tourist centres in the south of Bali and in Denpasar. Officially, all taxis must be equipped with a meter but many drivers refuse use them. If this happens, it is best to look for another taxi. The most reputable operator is **Blue Bird Taxi**, easily identifiable by their light-blue colour and blue bird on the roof. Their vehicles are by far the best maintained and safest, the drivers usually speak English and are trustworthy (that is the reason that many foreigners who live on Bali only take a Blue Bird taxi at night); the drivers usually turn the meter on without being asked to do so.
- The **prices** are low with the basic charge around Rp7,000 and then Rp6,500 per kilometre (0.6mi) and Rp50,000 per hour of waiting. Taxis can be ordered by telephone in the south of Bali (tel: 0361 70 11 11), alternatively you can download the My Blue Bird app (www.bluebirdgroup.com, available for Android and iOS).

Bemos and *Ojeks*

- ***Bemos***, which are also often called "Colts", are minibuses or converted vans with seats in the cargo area. They operate only along fixed routes between the towns and villages. Although they can only accommodate a dozen passengers at the most, they often have many more people on board. There is normally a conductor who calls out the destination and collects the fares; a route of about 10km (6mi) costs ca. Rp5,000. If you want to get off, you have to knock on the roof of the vehicle and call out "kiri" at the top of your voice. If aren't heard, you will have to try an even louder "kiri, kiri!"
- If you are in a real hurry, and have nerves of steel, you can jump onto the pillion seat of an *ojek*. Nothing is faster that these motorcycle taxis – and with a little luck, you might even reach your destination in one piece (a helmet will help). The **prices** vary greatly but are rarely lower than Rp4,000 per kilometre (0.6mi).

Accommodation

Imagine sleeping in a tree house and being awakened by the sound of monkeys calling. Or perhaps you like the idea of a luxurious teak villa with private pool and butler, a romantic beach hut straight out of *Robinson Crusoe*, a cosy guesthouse offering insights into Balinese daily life or a stylish glass villa on the slopes below a volcano? On Bali you will be spoilt for choice.

Reservations

- The **range of places to stay** on Bali may be extremely wide but they all have one thing in common: excellent value for money. And that is regardless of your price range.
- Viewing the accommodation before you make your reservation can only be recommended in the budget category, in the mid-category and especially in the top hotels online advance booking will get you a **bargain price**, often as much as 50 per cent off the standard rate.
- The booking can either take place on the website of the specific hotel or on one of the special **bookings websites** that frequently have even better offers (including www.balihotels.com; www.agoda.com; www.booking.com; www.hrs.com; www.expedia.com and many other sites).
- You can even save money by booking a **package holiday**, as the top hotels are often included at unbeatable prices.
- During the **high season** from June to August, as well as in the holiday season at the end of the year, it's often difficult to find a room in the holiday resorts on the island without an advance reservation. It is not unusual for accommodation prices in Kuta and Sanur to be increased by up to 50 per cent during these periods.

Accommodation Prices

Expect to pay per double room per night:

£ under Rp750,000

££ Rp750,000–1.5 million

£££ over Rp1.5 million

Guesthouses & Hotels

- Guesthouses, which are known as ***losmen*** or ***homestay*** on Bali, are by far the most economical places to stay. In most cases, the rooms are basic but clean and are furnished with a bed, mosquito net and fan. There is often a modest bathroom with cold running water – all you need in the tropics – as well as a veranda where a simple breakfast is served. This usually consists of banana pancakes, fruit salad and tea or coffee. The atmosphere is very relaxed and you will be able to get an insight into Balinese daily life. Your hosts might even invite you to festivals and other celebrations and it is an easy way to come into contact with the locals, as well as other tourists. And, all of this at prices from around Rp115,000 – even in the holiday centres. Some of the guesthouses even offer all the comforts of a hotel.

- The standard of accommodation that is classified as a **hotel**, often located in the midst of an exotic tropical garden, ranges from mediocre to incomparably luxurious. Many are built in the style of a villa, elaborately decorated with handicrafts and antiques and often so tasteful that you may want to stay forever.
- Of course, there are also ugly **concrete buildings** but they are few and far between on Bali where there are more than 100,000 hotel beds and probably at least as many in guesthouses, but almost no high-rise hotels.

Food and Drink

The adage that the way to a man's heart is through his stomach is especially true in Indonesia, where there are supposedly 1,600 specific dishes. The basis for most meals is steamed white rice and this is even incorporated in the standard greeting of "Sudah makan nasi?" meaning "Have you eaten rice today?"

From Food Stalls to Restaurants

- It is impossible to know just how many food stalls there are on Bali. Since the Balinese like to eat in the cooler evening hours, there are **night markets (*pasar malam*)** everywhere with rows of mobile food carts (*kaki lima*). You can have your soup at one, grab a snack at another and try the curry or a fish dish somewhere else. A satisfying selection of dishes will seldom cost more than Rp15,000 (ca. £0.85).
- It is also possible to have a filling meal in one of the many ***warungs*** – permanent food stalls with a table and two benches front and a protective awning – where dishes start at about Rp15,000.
- If you double this amount, you can move to a ***pumah makan***, a simple "eating house" equipped with a few tables (and maybe a fan) where you can usually choose from several different dishes.
- You can expect an even greater choice and more elaborate furnishing in a ***restoran.*** This is where Balinese or Indonesian cuisine is celebrated – in many different standards – and this also where you will often find European food, or food adapted to European tastes. Fried egg on toast, omelette, spaghetti and sandwiches have now all become standard fare and theses dishes are sometimes even eaten by the Balinese themselves.
- In the tourist centres – but not exclusively – you will also find standard **restaurants** offering a variety of cuisines in all possible price categories. There are also gourmet restaurants and Ubud, Seminyak and Jimbaran are gastronomic hotspots.

Restaurant Prices

Expect to pay per person for a main course, excluding drinks and service:

£ under Rp60,000
££ Rp60,000–120,000
£££ over Rp120,000

Spices to Tickle your Taste Buds

- The **diversity** of Indonesian cuisine – with influences from India, China and Malaysia – has earned it a reputation as one of the best in the world. And, it is also one of the healthiest.
- The cuisine is very **spicy** with many standard dishes flavoured with turmeric, coriander, bergamot and nutmeg, garlic, pepper, ginger and cloves, cardamom, lemon grass and mint. These are the most important spices and herbs but let us not forget about the fiery chilli peppers, which make Indonesian cuisine one of the worlds **hottest**.
- When you first arrive on Bali, you might find the exotic, hot spices are difficult to get used to but you will soon discover how tasty it can be. In addition, the Balinese also know that most tourists prefer a **milder version** of most dishes and the spiciness is usually reduced for foreigners. You will often be asked: "*bisa (makan) pedas* – can you eat spicy food?" If you answer *ya* (yes), be prepared for fireworks; a *tidak* (no) will spare your palate from a fiery onslaught. If you want comfortable balance, just say *sedikit* (a little). And, as soon as you have adapted to the traditional meal with plenty of rice, soups and other milder dishes you will give your palate the chance to experience many new taste sensations.
- Soup is served together with the meal (and not before or on its own), in contrast to the Western sequence of courses, all of the dishes, including the rice, are served at the same time at an Indonesian-Balinese meal. And, if you are eating with others, it is common practice for everybody to share what is on the table.

Meals

- A typical main meal, which is usually eaten in the **evening**, naturally consists of **rice** (*nasi*), seeing that, in Indonesian, "eating" is the same as "eating rice". This is accompanied by ***bakso***, a hearty clear soup with meatballs, or ***soto sayur*** (vegetable soup), a cooked dish such as ***rendang*** (beef curry), or ***opor ayam*** (chicken in coconut milk), a baked dish, often with ***ayam*** (chicken) or ***babi*** (pork) and – very frequently – ***sate*** (meat skewers). Sometimes a ***gado gado*** is also served, a warm salad of steamed vegetables with a creamy peanut sauce. The dessert is the only course that is served after the actual meal and – appropriately for a tropical paradise – it is fruit.
- Only light dishes are eaten at **midday**, when appetites decrease with the heat, dishes such as ***nasi goreng*** (fried rice with pieces of meat, some vegetables and possibly fried egg) or ***bami goreng*** (the same but with noodles instead of fried rice) or a soup such as the sweet and sour ***gedang mehuah*** made with green papaya.
- And of course a traditional **breakfast** on Bali is also a rice dish; either ***nasi putih*** (plain rice) with a ***telur*** (egg) or – as at noon or in the evening – with fried meat, vegetables and egg as ***nasi campur*** (rice with mixed dishes). Another popular dish is ***nasi lemak*** (coconut rice) is but nothing beats ***pisang goreng***, fried or battered bananas.

Shopping

People who enjoy shopping will be in seventh heaven in Bali. The ingenuity and craftsmanship of the Balinese – as well as their talent for copying garments that you give them – fill the countless shops on the island with an endless supply of new creations.

What to Buy

- Regardless of whether they are made by the silversmiths in Celuk (➤84), the stonemasons in Batubulan (➤83), the wood carvers in Mas (➤85), the painters in Ubud (➤75) and Batuan (➤85), the basket weavers and umbrella makers in Sukawati (➤85) or the weavers in Tenganan (➤113) – all the **handicrafts** produced on the island are available in the shops in the tourist centres. In addition, that is where you will also be able to purchase artefacts from the other islands in the Indonesian archipelago such as blowpipes from Kalimantan, wooden figures from Nias, batiks and shadow-puppets from Java, batak calendars from Sumatra, sarongs from Flores, penis sheaths from Irian Jaya and the list goes on.
- Since the old hippie community left Ibiza years ago and moved to Bali, where they became active in the **fashion** business, the shops are overflowing with all kinds of designer clothes. There are shirts and pants, T-shirts and dresses, skirts and jackets, so you are sure to find what you are looking for. And, you can have clothes tailor-made in silk or cotton for very reasonable prices.

Where to Buy

- The hotspot for shopaholics in Bali is Kuta, specifically the trio of Kuta, Legian and Seminyak. Anybody who has ever bought something here will want to return time and time again. The hipster outfits, as well as completely new designs, found here are probably unique worldwide. Shopping at home is downright boring by comparison.
- But beware, no matter how much money you have in your wallet you will spend it all! And nowhere is that easier than in Kuta, where the high demand and even higher shop rentals make everything twice as expensive as anywhere else and – regardless of how doggedly you bargain – you will seldom be able to beat them down to something more reasonable. This applies to the small shops on Poppies Lane, the large department stores and the ultra-modern shopping malls that are currently all the rage.
- The best prices in **Kuta** can usually be found in the eponymous district where you might pick up some bargain brand name sportswear – especially from the surfing scene. Before buying you should inspect the goods closely as there are also **damaged goods** and many **fakes** on the shop shelves.
- Neighbouring **Legian** is well known for its tailor workshops. Take your favourite items of clothing and have them copied there. You can also take a photo as a guideline.
- **Seminyak** is the place to go to for – mainly expensive – goods including genuine antiques and other items that look like they are.
- To buy handicrafts and art, the best place to go is where they are produced, and not just in Kuta where the prices are inflated. Ubud is an excellent place to go to, especially the **Ubud Art Market** (➤95).

Finding Your Feet

- Sanur would really not have much to offer shoppers were it not for the **Sanur Night Market**, which has earned a good reputation in recent years.
- Pamphlets in **Nusa Dua** promise a high-end shopping experience at the Bali Collection. However, some visitors will feel that the super-cool atmosphere of this "Instant Bali" is too sterile – you will either love it or hate it.
- **Street vendors** are omnipresent in the tourist centres and always seem to be where you happen to be. You can't escape them, let alone scare them off – it is pointless to shout at them or simply ignore them. Yes, they usually have outrageous prices, are annoying and a real nuisance, but you may behave in the same way if you lived in a $12m^2$ ($130ft^2$) one-room flat with six children, had no work and no chance of getting a job. So try to be polite even if you do not want to buy sarongs, shell necklaces, sunglasses, colourful shawls and all the other items they are trying to sell.

The Art of Haggling

- On Bali, you never know what an item will cost, there are **no fixed prices** and everything is settled by a negotiation. The only person who knows the real price is the seller and the buyer has to attempt to come as close to this as possible. But, this uncertainty is part of the excitement of haggling because the buyer always ends up feeling that they have made a good deal.
- There is a real **art** to not being taken for a ride. This is made even more difficult by the fact that there is not one single price for goods but many – there are different prices for people living in the city or countryside, for locals and foreigners, for the inquisitive and cautious, for the poor and rich, for men and women. Prices even vary depending on the time of day or day of the week, the seller's mood, for one article, two or more…There are just as many prices as there are situations.

- The most important rule of thumb – and this applies no matter what the seller says – is that the buyer should never make the first offer. The seller always makes the first price and the buyer then tries to get a **discount of at least 50%**. Failing that, you are guaranteed to have paid too much.

Entertainment

Bali is the perfect place for those who want to take a holiday from holidaying. Whether you want to spend a day, a night or three weeks with round-the-clock action, you will not be bored. Partygoers will head for Kuta and the only other place with a comparable nightlife is on Lombok's neighbouring island of Gili Trawangan. If you want a more active holiday, you will find more than enough to keep you busy on Bali.

Nightlife

- The nightlife in **Kuta** is legendary. Year after year, young people – mainly Australians – spend their whole holiday, or long weekends here and party through the night into the dawn. This mecca for holidaymakers is also very trendy and draws the affluent crowd from Jakarta and Singapore, as well as Koreans, Japanese and Chinese.

- After the sunsets below the horizon in a spectacular blaze of colour, Kuta's nightlife awakens. First of all in the restaurants, pubs and bars and then, around midnight, in the **countless clubs**, which compete with each other to be the hippest venue with famous international DJs, until the early hours of the morning. The epicentre of the nightlife in Kuta is the **party strip Jl. Legian.** This is the area with the greatest concentration of bars and clubs, including all of the classics that established Kuta's reputation as a nightlife capital. These include the **Bounty Discotheque** (➤ 67), the **Engine Room** (➤ 68) and the **Sky Garden Lounge** (➤ 68) all of which have constantly changing entertainment programmes featuring fire-eaters, dancers, acrobats and cover bands.
- The nightlife is quieter and calmer the closer one gets to **Legian,** and in **Seminyak** the nights are spent in stylish lounges, Bohemian cocktail bars and chic beach clubs such as the famous **Ku De Ta** (➤ 68). There is no better place to chill as the night wears on, that is as long as you have the necessary wherewithal and appropriate outfit as the bouncers are very selective in Seminyak.
- Compared with Kuta, the nightlife in all the other tourist centres on Bali is practically non-existent. The only alternative for people looking for some new fun is to take a speedboat across to **Gili Trawangan**. This is a meeting place for young backpackers from all over the world and it has a vibrant nightlife. On Monday, the Blue Marlin's psychedelic and techno beats draws the crowd to rave on the dance floor; on Wednesday, there is hip-hop and house in the Tir na Nog; Fridays belong to Rudy's Pub where trance and techno blasts out and reggae fans can have fun in the Sama Sama Bar every night of the week. A party boat sets out on a laid-back trip around the Gili Islands everyday at 10am. And, once a month, everyone goes wild at the **Gili Trawangan Full Moon Party**. It does not come close to the more famous Ko Pha Ngan Full Moon Party but it is a pretty good alternative!

Being Active in Bali

- Relaxing and looking at temples is all well and good but you may want to do more than that. There are so many options if you want to be physically active on Bali – on land and in the water – that it comes as no surprise that glossy magazines promote the island as being a paradise for nature lovers, sports enthusiasts and adventurer seekers. The possibilities are almost limitless and no other holiday destination in Southeast Asia can boast a comparable **infrastructure,** or offer better prices.
- However, tourists will search in vain for beaches that are suitable for **swimming** in Bali as, contrary to the popular opinion, Bali is not a bathing island in the usual sense. Along the unprotected southern coast there is often huge surf and very dangerous currents, at Sanur and Nusa Dua the tide goes out so far that it is impossible to swim, while the north coast does have some options where you can swim but there are coral reefs. And, the grey and black lava beaches are also not as visually attractive.
- The miles of coral reef off the north coast near **Amed, Tulamben** and **Lovina** are ideal for **snorkelling** as is the east coast – especially

around **Padang Bai** and **Nusa Lembongan**. However, the coral gardens that are part of the protected marine area of **Pulau Menjangan** are unparalleled and also perfectly suited for diving. The small island enjoys a reputation for being one of the most spectacular dive spots in Southeast Asia (although the coral banks off Lombok's neighbouring island of Gili Trawangan are just as worthy of this superlative).

- The range of other **water sports** could not be more varied and includes rafting through the unspoilt wilderness, kayak trips on wild rivers, boat trips, sailing cruises and parasailing.
- **Surfing** is another main attraction and Bali's surf spots are internationally famous. Most of the surfers ride beach breaks in and around **Kuta** but **Balian** and **Medewi** further to the west are also popular surf destinations. The small beach bays on the **Bukit Badung** Peninsula are infamous for the sheer size of the waves and the danger of its famed surf breaks.
- Two volcanoes, **Gunung Batur** and **Gunung Agung**, dominate the island's interior and climbing these sacred mountains is a double highlight. At a height of 1,717m (5,633ft), Gunung Batur is a relatively quick and easy climb while Gunung Agung, the Balinese version of Mount Olympus, soars up 3,142m (10,308ft). Both reward the effort with spectacular volcanic landscapes and panoramic views that are unmatched in Southeast Asia.
- Those keen on **hiking,** will experience unforgettable views of volcanoes, crater lakes and waterfalls, rain, fog and even monkey forests. Spectacular landscapes and an authentic impression of the country and the people are also guaranteed for all those who decide to go on a bicycle tour. Almost the whole island is suitable for cycling, with the exception of the southern part of Denpasar.
- **Golfers** on Bali will enjoy the privilege of teeing off at golf courses in beautiful locations. In the highlands of Bedugul there is the **Bali Handara Golf Course** with colourful flora as well as the 18-hole **Bali Golf & Country Club**, which is right on the Indian Ocean.
- In the island's interior, and along the coasts, there are **wellness and spa resorts** that offer relaxation for the body and soul. There are several dozen in Kuta alone and there are even more in Ubud. Treatments include massages, Ayurveda, fasting courses, meditation exercises, yoga, reiki and tea ceremonies, as well as shamanistic practices, healing, Qigong, channelling, palm reading, numerology and much more.

The South

Little Treats

In the Wind

Pantai Mersari in **Sanur** (➤ 61) is a meeting place for kite surfers – just watching can be fun.

Spectacle at Dawn

The early bird gets the worm...and if you are lucky you may even have the sunrise at the **Pura Luhur Ulu Watu** (➤ 50) all to yourself.

Bird Market

The atmosphere at Denpasar's **Tanah Lapang Puputan** (➤ 60) bird market is absolutely authentic – but this is definitely not for animal lovers.

Getting Your Bearings

The south of Bali is by far the most visited part of the island. Here you find Indonesia's version of the Copacabana, as well as picturesque bays and the island's best surfing conditions. There are no limits to the attractions waiting for water sport enthusiasts and night owls. And, the great infrastructure of many of the holiday resorts guarantees a comfortable and varied stay.

The fishermen in southern Bali still set out to sea in traditional boats

In the 1970s, backpackers from Western countries and surfers from Australia discovered southern Bali. Just a few years later, this insider's tip was no longer a secret and today 5 million foreign visitors visit southern Bali every year, making this tropical paradise the most popular island in Indonesia. And, whether the waves and beaches, the sundowners and sunsets, the vibrant nightlife and the culinary highlights, the Balinese, the temples and the tropical heat seduce them – they all agree that southern Bali is absolutely unique.

There is something for all tastes on Bali. While Kuta, with Legian and Seminyak, forms the hip surfer and party mecca of the island (and is definitely ahead when it comes to nightlife and fun), Sanur presents itself as a (package) holiday centre for the more sedate clientele looking for a peaceful blend of beach life, culture and affordable comfort. Nusa Dua, on the other hand, is synonymous with luxury tourism while Jimbaran is a relaxed – but very expensive – beach oasis that fits in with the standard Bali cliché. The island's metropolis Denpasar is only a few kilometres away from all of these holiday resorts. And, if you feel like escaping from the hustle and bustle of the tourist centres, you can go on excursions to the temples on the cliffs and sea in the south, where you will experience the most spectacular sunsets imaginable.

Surfer's paradise Indonesian style – the conditions around Kuta are perfect

TOP 10

2 Pura Tanah Lot ➤ 48
6 Pura Luhur Ulu Watu ➤ 50
10 Kuta ➤ 53

Don't Miss

(11) Jimbaran ➤ 56
(12) Bukit Badung ➤ 58

At Your Leisure

(13) Denpasar ➤ 60
(14) Sanur ➤ 61
(15) Nusa Dua ➤ 62

The South

Two Perfect Days

You will definitely need two days to see southern Bali's main attractions – the temples, beaches and the entire holiday hustle and bustle. And, if you do not want to miss the magnificent sunsets on the two evenings, you must keep your eye on the clock during the afternoon. A rental car, with or without driver, is the best way to get around.

Day 1

Morning

You should plan on taking the whole morning if you want to even get an overview of 14 **Sanur** (➤ 61) and/or 10 **Kuta** (➤ 53). You shouldn't expect any sights in the classical sense of the word but there is more than enough waiting to be discovered in the boutiques and souvenir shops and – of course – on the beaches; you will certainly not to be bored.

Lunch

Exploring holiday centres can be strenuous – when you reach the west end of Kuta, you will probably want to relax and have something to eat and drink and there is no better place to do so than in **Ku De Ta** (➤ 68). Here you can recover from all your holiday exertions and enjoy the cool, laid-back atmosphere.

Afternoon

Half an hour's drive from Seminyak is the scenic sea temple of 2 **Pura Tanah Lot** (➤ 48; above) with its spectacular location. You should try to arrive by around 3pm as from around 4pm busloads of tourists start arriving. They push and shove their way towards the temple and you will no longer get much of a feeling for the real atmosphere of this sacred placed.

Evening

The Tanah Lot light show, which can be admired from the observation terrace, begins after 5:30pm. The sun recedes slowly and the "grand finale", when the sunset sinks below the waves is at around 6pm. A few minutes later most of the visitors take to their heels. However, it is well worth lingering for another half an hour or so. And when the almost mystical atmosphere returns as the area is bathed in twilight. When you have seen enough, head back to 10 **Kuta** (➤ 53), which is the best option for a meal and to soak up the atmosphere.

Day 2

Morning

The beach at 11 **Jimbaran** (➤ 56) is often even more beautiful in the early hours of the morning than at sunset. Set out as early as possible (10am at the latest) so that you can drive via 15 **Nusa Dua** (➤ 62) to your favourite beach at 12 **Bukit Badung** (➤ 58).

Afternoon

You could spend the entire holiday on the surfing and bathing beaches of Bukit Badung but initially a couple of hours have to suffice. You should leave the last bathing beach by 4pm and continue your journey towards 6 **Pura Luhur Ulu Watu** (➤ 50).

Evening

At around 6pm you can see the spectacle of the sunset and the dance performances which begin about one hour later at 7pm. You should let the day come to an end with a candlelight dinner on the beach at 11 **Jimbaran** (➤ 56; below); our recommendation there is the **Muaya Beach** (➤ 56).

2 Pura Tanah Lot

Countless Bali brochures are adorned with glossy photographs of Pura Tanah Lot rising out of the shallow water in front of a glowing orange sky. This dramatic spectacle of nature with the silhouette of the sea temple at sunset takes place just off the Indian Ocean coast and is definitely one of the most memorable highlights of any trip to Bali.

The sea temple can only be accessed at low tide

There is also statistical proof of this as more than 2 million visitors – 1 million of them foreign tourists – visit the Tanah Lot temple every year. This is a record on Bali and in Indonesia as a whole; and, as it is a well-known fact that tourism increases in proportion to the number of tourists, you can imagine how this famous, **most visited and photographed shrine** on the island follows the laws of marketing.

At around 4pm rush hour begins at the culture park, between the car park and temple. Along with thousands of other visitors you will have to struggle your way through the labyrinth of vendors and stalls that line the path to the **panoramic cliffs** and the temple complex. However, don't be put off by all of the pushing and shoving, when the hour approaches and the sun starts sinking in a blaze of colour, even the most cantankerous of critics are silenced and awed by the beauty of it all. If you want to watch the sunset without too many "obstacles" in front of you, you should try to arrive before 4pm and secure a place with the best panoramic view.

Insider Tip

Sacred Healing

The sunset is the actual highlight as the temple itself – like all temples on Bali – is off limits for tourists and can only be entered by devout Hindus. In any case, this is also only possible at low tide. And, only then is it possible for the priest to show the sacred **fresh water spring** that bubbles up at the foot of the island rock. The water is believed to have healing powers; people who want to drink have to give the guard a small donation – it should be at last Rp10,000. The same applies on the opposite shore where a priest guards a **small cave**, which houses sacred and highly poisonous, black-and-white striped sea snakes.

TAKING A BREAK

There are numerous refreshment stands and several restaurants. However, the food is overpriced in all of them. The **Warung Segara** (tel: 0361 81 08 26; daily 8am–7pm) near the observation terrace has front-row seats where you can watch the sunset.

190 B3 Tanah Lot
0361 88 03 61; www.tanahlot.net
Daily 8am–7pm
Rp30,000, car park: Rp5,000

INSIDER INFO

- An updated **calendar of events** is available on the temple website www.tanahlot.net. The temple is frequently visited by thousands of pilgrims when festivals take place.
- After sunset, **Balinese dance dramas** are performed in the culture park every evening from 7pm (admission Rp90,000).

Pura Luhur Ulu Watu

It is an unforgettable experience to see the magnificent panorama from the "temple on the rock" to the sea surging against the coast 100m (330ft) below. Even if you were not able to see the neighbouring island of Java (60km/37mi in the distance), which is possible on clear days.

Its position on an impressive steep cliff high above the **southwestern tip of the Bukit Badung Peninsula** (➤ 58) is what makes the Pura Luhur Ulu Wat so unique. Insider Tip This is the southernmost and – as many believe – most spectacular point on the entire island. The setting is quite simply unique – especially at sunset. This also means that, just like **Pura Tanah Lot** (➤ 48), it is very crowded, but this should not stop you from visiting.

World Balance

The history of the temple dates back to the 11th century. The reason for its establishment is the very cliff on which the temple is located. According to legend, it embodies

The Pura Luhur Ulu Watu is a popular subject for photographs – but beware the monkeys who are wild about cameras and mobile phones

the petrified ship on which the goddess of lakes and rivers, **Dewi Danu**, sailed across the sea to Bali to protect the island from the forces of the underworld. The Balinese consider the sea to be the home of spirits and demons. It is necessary to placate them with offerings in order to maintain cosmic harmony, the balance between good and evil. This explains the significance of this temple, which is responsible for preventing the forces of evil lurking in the depths of the ocean from climbing out onto the land. And, because this task is too great for a single temple, it shares the work with Pura Tanah Lot (➤ 48). That is why, together with this temple and right after the mother temple Besakih (➤ 104), it is the most sacred on the island.

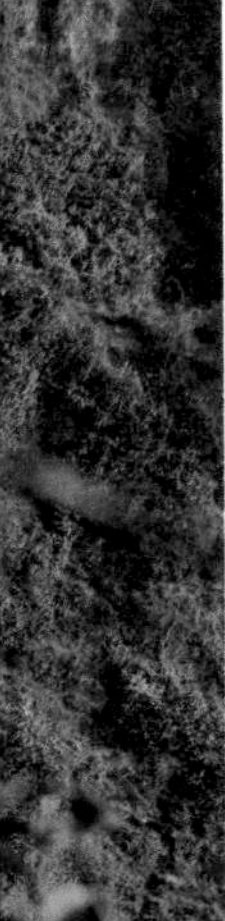

Beware, Monkeys!

The steep staircase leading up 70 steps to the temple's **entrance portal** is decorated with the heads of demons. However, monkey heads would be more appropriate; dozens – if not hundreds – of long-tailed **macaques** get up to mischief with tourists here and steal anything that is not nailed down. This also happens in the monkey forests in Ubud (➤ 76) and Sangeh (➤ 92), where you should take special care of glasses, cameras and mobile phones. Insider Tip If you feel the urge to stroke one of the seemingly friendly animals – which many unsuspecting tourists seem to feel they must – beware; you might be bitten faster than you can pull your hand back! And feeding the monkeys means that you will have a hard time getting away from them no matter how hard you try…

Uplifting and Beautiful

After entering the temple, you will find yourself in the **forecourt** that, similar to the **first and second courtyards**, is enclosed with coral stones. It is not permitted to go any further forward as only the faithful may enter the Holy of Holies (as is the case with all temples on Bali). However, the boundary wall is low enough for you to be able to get a good view of everything and – most important – take excellent photographs. The view over the **cliff** down to the Indian Ocean with more than 10m (33ft) high waves thundering against it on three sides is absolutely breathtaking.

TAKING A BREAK

The **modest *warungs*** at the car park below the temple serve cold beverages and simple meals. However, they are not really very attractive. A more stylish way to end the sunset tour to the temple is with a culinary and atmospheric highlight – a candlelight dinner on the beach at **Jimbaran** (➤ 56).

---

190 B1 **Bukit Badung**
Daily 7am–7pm
Rp30,000, car park Rp5,000

INSIDER INFO

Insider Tip

- If you want to avoid the packed crowds in the area near the temple, but still enjoy the fabulous panoramic view, you should take the **narrow footpath**, which leads from the temple a short distance to the south to another cliff. There, you will often have the view all for yourself and – another advantage – the silhouette of the temple as a photogenic cutout behind you, at least at sunset.
- At this latitude sunset is always around 6pm. A dance performance begins in the amphitheatre near the temple at the same time (Rp90,000). The extremely colourful **Kecak** monkey dance (below) is performed every evening illuminated by dozens of tar torches and it is extremely photogenic. The best places to take photographs are in the upper rows. However, you should be sure to buy your tickets an hour before the performance begins because these rows are very popular and from 5:30pm there is a run on the ticket booths.

10 Kuta

There is no better place in Indonesia for night owls and party animals than Bali's most famous tourist triangle of Kuta-Legian-Seminyak. The three erstwhile villages are located on what is by the far the longest and also most beautiful sandy beach on the island. The villages have merged to form one single holiday resort that stretches for around 7km (4.5mi) along the coast. It has the reputation of being the most vibrant package tourism holiday destination in all of Southeast Asia. If you are looking for the tourist heart of Bali, you will find it here.

And it has been like that since the late 1960s when the first backpackers, surfers and self-proclaimed hippies arrived in Kuta. By the 1980s, Kuta (which had grown into a city by then) and the neighbouring village of Legian

The beach sections at Seminyak are a little classier

had become the most popular spot in Asia for backpackers and surfers. Then in the 1990s, the long stretch of seaside between Kuta and Legian developed into a mass-tourism goldmine. It has since taken hold of Seminyak, which borders on Legian, in a more luxurious variant. It can be assumed that the beaches and villages further to west will soon follow suit. An end to the boom is not in sight, as tourism to Bali continues unabated.

As a result of this, there have been some ugly developments – especially in construction – and people who knew the area in the past would be shocked to see it now and would perhaps feel that Bali has made a big error in judgement. The palm groves lining the extremely wide sandy beach have long since given way to a boulevard and towering concrete blocks, and expensive resorts have replaced the simple palm-leaf roofed huts. And, the hours of solitude on the beach are very much a thing of the past, as you now have to share the beach with thousands of others.

Three Places, One Destination

But Kuta is not just Kuta and this means that all kinds of holidaymakers will find exactly what they are looking for during their holiday. The Kuta district tends to be the domain of the young, hip party crowd from Australia. After dancing and drinking all night long, they often go to bed around dawn, get up late, go shopping, to the beach or surfing, before the whole cycle starts all over again. The cost of accommodation and other facilities are at the lower end of the price scale.

The exact opposite is true of **Seminyak**; this resort appeals to the young and the beautiful, and those with a little bit more money to spend. Although they go to the beach from time to time, they generally to prefer to say around their exquisite pool landscapes. These top-notch hotels are located, like oases of peace and tranquillity, between the rice fields on the one side and the main street with its chic boutiques on the other. In the evening, visitors stroll along Jl. Laksmana, the main boulevard, to see and be seen and then head off to savour the culinary highlights in one of the wickedly expensive restaurants before partying the night away in one of the elegant nightclubs.

Legian lies in the middle of these two extremes; it is both a laid-back party venue and stylish area with gourmet restaurants. Backpackers are few and far between – and so are luxury tourists – as most of the accommodation available is in the mid-price range.

The Beach

The beach stretches out continuously to the west, as far as the horizon. It is wide with fine sand that shimmers in shades of gold and grey (depending on the current) and is watched over by *Baywatch*-style lifeguards. The water near the shore is shallow and ideal for splashing around in but less suited for swimming due the surging – often metre-high – waves. The surf in the Kuta section attracts body boarders and surfers and this is also where you will find the most bathers and sun worshippers surrounded by countless local beach hawkers and vendors. The closer you get to Seminyak, the larger the distance between beach towels and deckchairs.

SEX ON THE BEACH

This might be fine for a cocktail but it should definitely not be practiced in the literal sense. Indonesian law is strict and punishes such disrespectful behaviour with a prison sentence and subsequent deportation. But that still has little or no deterrent effect as every year one or more couples are caught in the act on the beach in Kuta, and then have to pay the price.

Kuta's beach is firmly in the hands of surfers, who ride its waves until nightfall

TAKING A BREAK

There is almost no limit to the possibilities but those who want to join the "in" crowd should head to **Ku De Ta** (➤ 68) at least once. It is right on the beach at Seminyak and it's a great place to sip a glass of freshly squeezed fruit juice. The chic beach club is also *the* trendiest spot for a sundowner and you can dine on the top-quality Asian-Italian fusion cuisine and then, later in the evening, it is the perfect place to chill out. Assuming, that is, that you have the necessary wherewithal!

190 C2

Bali Government Tourist Information Centre
Century Plaza Building Jl. Benesari 7, Kuta
0361 75 40 90 Daily 9am–9pm

Perama Tours & Travel
Jl. Legian 39, Kuta 0361 75 15 51; www.peramatour.com

INSIDER INFO

- The stretch of beach will seem endless if you **walk** from Kuta to Pura Tanah Lot, which is about 20km (12.5mi) away. The beach doesn't end until the western tip of the island.
- **Topless bathing** is frowned on in Bali – it is only tolerated on the beach at Kuta and nowhere else on the island.
- The offshore **currents**, as well as the surging waves, make this stretch of beach dangerous for swimmers. Unfortunately, never a month goes by without a drowning victim. You should pay particular attention to the **warning flags** and only go into the water if they are yellow and never swim if when the red or black flags are up!

11 Jimbaran

Once a fishing village and now a holiday resort, Jimbaran is a peaceful – but pricey – beach oasis, one which most closely matches the popular Bali cliché.

The 4km (2.5mi) crescent of **Jimbaran Bay** flanks the west side of the small isthmus that connects the Balinese "mainland" to the Bukit Badung Peninsula. A coral reef protects the sandy beach from waves and currents so the sea is often as smooth as glass and the beach's gentle slope also makes it perfect for swimming. Fishing boats and beach umbrellas add splashes of colour, the sea shimmers in shades of blue and, if the weather is fine, the silhouettes of all the island's volcanoes complete the picture-perfect tropical image. Beach enthusiasts will be happy to hear that many tourists prefer the pool at their luxury hotels and rarely make their way to the beach, so the beach is often nearly empty.

Sunset Dinner with your Feet in the Sand

There is therefore no shortage of space for your towel or for long beach walks and it is not until dusk that the sleepy atmosphere suddenly changes up a gear. One minute the beach will be empty then, in next to no time, elegant tables are quickly set up for luxurious sunset seafood barbecues. Coconut fires are lit and, and before you know, all the places are occupied by several dozen restaurants and their tables are full of well-dressed connoisseurs of good food, who are also rather generous. Much to the delight of the musicians, who wander from table to table, entertaining the guests between courses. Traditional dances are also performed at some locations and – as the night moves on – fire shows are occasionally on the programme, although they are no competition for the spectacular sunsets.

TAKING A BREAK

On Jimbaran Beach, the **Jimbaran Food Court** is a good choice for refreshments, snacks or a reasonably priced lunch. It is at the southern end of the sandy beach road, Pantai Kedonganan.

190 C2

At sunrise Jimbaran Beach still looks like an idyllic fishing village

INSIDER INFO

To indulge in some seafood at sunset on Jimbaran Beach, but without breaking your budget, you should head to the southern section of the beach, near the Intercontinental Hotel. To get there, take Jl. Bukit Permai, which branches off from the main road Jl. Raya Uluwatu. There, at **Muaya Beach**, the evenings are all about seafood but the prices are far more reasonable – and often half the price that they are on Jimbaran Beach itself.

BALI 03

12 Bukit Badung

In the far south of Bali, the coral limestone plateau of the drop-shaped Bukit Badung Peninsula juts out into the Indian Ocean. It has two aspects: to the east, where Nusa Dua (➤ 62) is also located, a safe and rather sterile Bali while to the west, with Pura Luhur Ulu Watu (➤ 50), the scenery is wilder, more romantic, with many small sandy coves at the foot of the steep cliffs.

These bays are where the best, and most daring, surfers paddle out to sea. These big wave riders are the only ones who are able tackle **Asia's highest and most dangerous waves**. Monster waves build up off beyond the razor-sharp coral reefs that run parallel to the coast. And, since high waves usually go hand in hand with strong currents, swimmers enjoying the good conditions just off the beach should always be extremely careful.

As there are no lifeguards on the beaches, and **very little infrastructure**, you will almost feel like you have gone back to the good old days before the tourist resorts arrived on Bali. Accommodation is rustic, as are the *warungs*, and everything is largely geared towards the (minimal) needs of the surfers and backpackers, which are – with the exception of a few day-trippers – the main guests on these beaches.

With their simple wooden huts, the beaches in the west of the peninsula are still rather rustic (pictured below is Pantai Padang Padang)

Bathing Bays and Coves

The most northerly beach bay, the **Pantai Balangan**, is 6km (3.5mi) away from the main road to Ulu Watu, and it is signposted. It ends at the village of Balangan high above the sea, where you will also find a handful of mid-price resorts. Paths lead from there (20-minute walk) down to the sandy beach with a row of wooden *warungs*. They serve reasonably priced food and – even better – offer dirt-cheap accommodation. They have deckchairs and surfboards available to rent, there are surfing and yoga courses on offer and you can swim in the bay (only at high tide) but do exercise caution and stay close to the beach.

A short distance further to the south, and also signposted on the main road to Ulu Watu, is the small beach of **Pantai Bingin**, which lies at the base of a steep cliff. However, the strong currents here make for limited swimming. At the top of the cliff, you can overnight in mid-priced accommodation while there are also some cheap *warung* rooms on the beach. To the north is **Dreamland Beach**, which is mainly of interest to surfers, and to the south is **Impossible Beach** (its name is an indication of the waves there) and the long stretch of **Pantai Padang Padang**, with the obligatory wooden *warungs* for inexpensive meals and overnight stays.

This leaves **Pantai Suluban**, hidden between bizarre, eroded rocks more or less at the foot of Pura Luhur Uru Watu. A rough track leads down to the brilliant white sand beach with the crystal clear blue water. It is also possible to spend the night here (very reasonable prices) or on top of the cliff where things are more upmarket.

TAKING A BREAK

The small beach *warungs* are part and parcel of any bay and cove and they are the best – and far and away – cheapest choice for any meal. There are not many differences between them at Pantai Balangan, **Café Limo** has great Balinese fare and the food served at the **Sunset Café** is cheap and tasty.

---

190 C1

INSIDER INFO

After Jimbaran, on your way to the beach bays and to Pura Luhur Ulu Watu (► 50), you will see signposts to the **Garuda Wisnu Kencana Cultural Park** (Jl. Raya Uluwatu, Ungasan; tel: 0361 70 08 08; www.gwkbali.com; daily 8am–10pm; admission Rp100,000). The 60ha (150-acre) park was intended to showcase Balinese culture and be a place where tourists and the locals could mingle but it feels more like Disneyland. There is also a villa resort, restaurant with panoramic views and a well-stocked souvenir shop. The highlight of the complex, which has not yet been fully completed, is a 23m (75ft) statue of the god Vishnu. If work continues as planned, this should reach 120m (390ft) by 2018, which would make it the world's highest statue, taller than the Statue of Liberty in New York.

At Your Leisure

13 Denpasar

Some cities are easy to get to know, while others are more difficult for visitors. Denpasar falls into the second category, its population has doubled to 800,000 since 2000, and it continues to grow. It is quite simply a typical, large Asian city with all the associated issues: slum suburbs (that will soon extend to the holiday resorts in the south), completely congested streets, lots of noise, and exhaust fumes and rubbish, a hectic hustle and bustle. The only exotic feeling here is one of deprivation. However, there are a few sights that are of cultural and historic interest – it is up to you to decide whether it is worth braving the chaos to see them. In any case, you should definitely not attempt to drive to the city centre in your rental car. Endless traffic jams are the rule here, the signposting is a nightmare and, if you do not know the shortcuts, you might have to spend hours breathing in exhaust fumes in the sweltering heat. You should take a taxi to **Tanah Lapang Puputan**, this square is in the centre of the city and it is also where you will find the Puputan Monument. It is on the northern edge of the square (➤ 26) and commemorates the mass ritual suicide of the court of the Prince of Bandung in 1906.

A stone's throw away, on the south side of the square, are the four palatial buildings that form the **Bali Museum.** It was founded in 1932 by the Dutch as an art and ethnology museum, and documents the development of Balinese art and tradition from its beginnings to the present day. If you are interested in Balinese culture you should also visit the **Taman Budaya Art Center**, which is 2km (1.2mi) further to the east (take a taxi). Set in a large park (5ha/12 acres), the culture centre houses a Bali-baroque style museum dedicated to the history and art of the island. One highlight is the small special exhibition devoted to the work of the German artist Walter Spies (➤ 75), who lived in Ubud in the 1930s and had a huge influence on Balinese art. Reproductions of his paintings and photos are on display.

✚ 191 D3

The Bali Museum in Denpasar is as richly decorated as a Balinese temple

You have everything at your fingertips in Sanur, where the hotel gardens extend down to the beach

Denpasar Government Tourism Office
✉ Jl. Majapahit 1 ☎ 0361 8 49 57 07; www.balidenpasartourism.com
🕓 Mon–Thu 8am–3pm, Fri, Sat until 11am

Bali Museum
✉ Jl. Mayor Wisnu/Tanah Lapang Puputan
☎ 0361 22 26 80
🕓 Sat–Thu 8am–3:30pm, Fri until 11am
Rp15,000

Taman Budaya Art Center
✉ Jl. Nusa Indah ☎ 0361 22 71 76
🕓 Mon–Thu 8am–3pm, Fri–Sun 8am–11am
Rp15,000

14 Sanur

Sanur borders Denpasar to the west and will soon merge with the metropolis. It is a (package) holiday resort for a more mature clientele in search of a combination of beach, culture and affordable comfort. English is spoken widely and, although the first hotels were built here in the early 1960s, Sanur has managed to maintain a certain village character. It stretches for several kilometres along a coast lined by a pleasantly wide, sandy beach. This stretch is easily accessible by the **Jl. Tamblingan** road that runs parallel to the beach for around 5km (3mi). There is an endless row of boutiques and souvenir shops, restaurants, bars and other tourist facilities. Between the road and the sea are hotel complexes (mostly three- and four-star) set in park-like gardens.

There is a pedestrian promenade along the **beach** itself. An offshore **coral reef** protects the beach from waves and the sea here is usually as smooth as glass and ideal for children and older visitors. But only when the tide is high, at low tide the water sometimes recedes as far back as the reef.

At the northern end of the beach promenade is a museum well worth a visit. The **Museum Le Mayeur** is

READY FOR THE ISLANDS

Sanur and the harbour at Serangan, a little to the south of the holiday centre, are the best departure points for tourists who want to visit the island of **Gili Trawangan** (► 173) off the coast of Lombok, and/or the islands of **Nusa Lembongan** (► 118) and **Nusa Penida** (► 117) off Bali's east coast. Companies such as **Perama Tours & Travel** (Jl. Hang Tuah; tel: 0812 3 66 53 17; www.peramatour.com) offer daily connections to these islands.

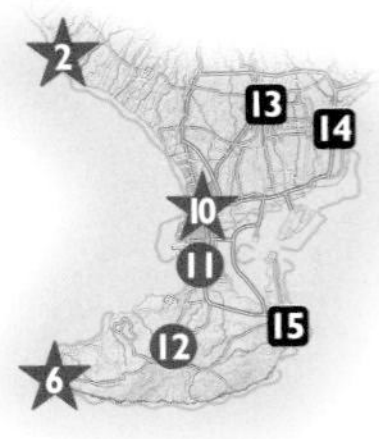

dedicated to the work of the Belgian artist Jean Le Mayeur who lived here from 1935 until his death in 1958. Several dozen paintings by the Impressionist are on display. Another attraction is the lush, flower-filled garden that surrounds the museum, which was previously the artist's home.

191 E2/3

Museum Le Mayeur
Jl. Hang Tuah 0361 28 62 01
Sat–Thu 8am–3pm, Fri 9am–noon
Rp10,000

15 Nusa Dua

Located on the northeast edge of the Bukit Badung Peninsula, Nusa Dua is a holiday resort with the capacity to accommodate more than 500,000 guests annually in its numerous high-end hotels. The luxurious oasis – that is as sterile as it is elegant – is the result of a master plan drawn up at the end of the 1970s with the aim of channelling the flow of tourists in order to protect Bali's culture from being damaged by uncontrolled growth. However, during this process the "real" Bali fell by the wayside and the resulting resort area is not everyone's cup of tea. Walls, security barriers and extremely strict security all protect the illustrious package tourists from coming into contact with the locals, so that they will not be disturbed while they play their cricket or golf. If culture is required – for example, in the form of Balinese dance dramas – it is brought directly into the hotel. In addition, a replica of a Balinese village was built in the **Nusa Dua Tourism Complex** for dining and shopping.

Even the beaches were imported – they are partially artificial – as the coral reefs extend up to the coast, guests have to wait for high tide if they want to go swimming in the sea rather than the hotel pools. Water sports are also available but the real water sports centre is outside of the enclave, a short distance away at the Tanjung Benoa resort, which is signposted on **Jl. Pratama**.

The palatial **Museum Pasifika Nusa Dua** was opened in Nusa Dua itself in 2006. It displays several hundred works by artists from around 25 countries in the Asia-Pacific region, as well as paintings by Western artists who have lived and worked in the area.

191 D1

Museum Pasifika Nusa Dua
Area Block P
0361 77 49 35; www.museum-pasifika.com
Daily 10am–6pm Rp70,000

The Hotel Amanusa (➤ 64) in Nusa Dua is a luxurious refuge

Where to... Stay

Accommodation Prices
Expect to pay per double room per night:
£ under Rp750,000 **££** Rp750,000–1.5 million **£££** over Rp1.5 million

BUKIT BADUNG

Balangan Paradise Hostel £

This hostel offers as much as a two-star hotel, and it also has a wonderful location right on the beach – you can't get any closer to the sea. The rooms are clean, air-conditioned, with bath/WC and balcony, around 25m² (270ft²) and a real bargain at only ca. £15. The complex does not have a website of its own so reservations must be made through one of the booking websites, such as www.booking.com.

190 C1
Jl. Pantai Balangan
0361 9 11 49 91

JIMBARAN

Keraton Jimbaran Beach Resort ££

Resorts on the beach in Jimbaran are generally unaffordable for ordinary mortals but the Keraton is an exception. Together with an elegant pool landscape, it occupies an excellent location in a well-maintained tropical garden right behind the beach, which is quite clean at this section. It has several restaurants and stylish, traditional Balinese rooms, which are ridiculously priced at less than £60. However, that rate only applies to reservations made through a hotel booking website; if you book on-site or via the hotel's website the starting rate is ca. £175. Insider Tip

190 C2
Jl. Majapati
0361 70 19 61; www.keratonjimbaranresort.com.

KUTA

Alaya Resort ££

The location of this brand new boutique hotel is ideal – it is close to the beach and centre but still pleasantly quiet. The same applies to the luxuriant garden, the good-sized pool and the exceptionally large rooms (45m²/485ft²). The rooms are elegant but unpretentious and are decorated in a Balinese style, and all have a balcony and comfortable seating area overlooking the garden.

190 C2
Jl. Kartika Plaza Gang Puspa Ayu 99
0361 75 53 80; www.alayahotels.com

Poppies Cottages I £££

Tourists who can afford to spend around £85 a night (2 persons, incl. breakfast) should do themselves a favour and book one of the two-dozen bungalows scattered throughout the wonderful tropical garden with an unusual pool landscape. The architecture skilfully interprets Balinese elements in a modern, contemporary fashion. Breakfast is served on the terraces of the cottages, which are elaborately decorated with Balinese arts and crafts; the resort's restaurant is one of the best and most popular in

town. It would also be hard to find a better the location, it is very central yet still peaceful, and the beach is only a few minutes' walk away. An oasis in Kuta!
190 C2 ✉ Poppies Lane 1
☎ 0361 75 10 59;
www.poppiesbali.com

The Kana Kuta £
It would be difficult to find better value for money in Kuta than this three-star hotel. The horseshoe-shaped, three-storey complex is built around a large swimming pool; it has two restaurants and a gym that overlooks the pool. The Kana Kuta has 96 pleasantly spacious (25m² /270ft²) rooms that are spotlessly clean. They all have tiled floors and good mid-range fittings and furnishing. All the rooms have balconies and the nicest ones are those with a view of the pool. The price of ca. £25 per night for two persons is a real steal. Guests can (and should) add another £4.5 and book their room with breakfast; the lavish buffet breakfast is really more than worth the small extra cost. Insider Tip
190 C2
✉ Jl. Setiabudi 8, Kuta district
☎ 0361 849 61 00; www.thekana.com

NUSA DUA

If you want to stay in Nusa Dua and not pay inflated prices, you should book a Bali package holiday – tourists who organise their own travel will have to pay considerably more per night, which is likely to dent the budget but if budget isn't an issue then whey not do it in style!

Amanusa £££
This has to be Bali's (possibly even Indonesia's) most luxurious accommodation – an elegant, award-winning, haven.
191 D1
☎ 0361 77 23 33;
www.aman.com/resorts/amanusa

SANUR

Hotel Jati & Home Stay £
Two people can spend the night here for less than £35, and even have a lavish breakfast served on the veranda of their private bungalow. It is impossible to find such comfort (and proximity to the beach) for this price elsewhere in Sanur. The charming cottages are either in the traditional Balinese style (very cosy) or a more modern variant. They all have a view of a small pool and are equipped with air conditioning, a fan and mosquito nets. They are in great demand so you will need reserve well in advance – it is considerably cheaper to make your reservation through a booking website than it is via the hotel's own website.
191 E2/3
✉ Jl. Danau Tamblingan 168
☎ 0361 28 17 30;
www.hoteljatiandhomestay.com

Hotel Puri Tempo Doeloe ££
This exceptionally well maintained garden property is a 15-minute walk from the beach (but there is also a free shuttle service). This is a good way to save money because you would have to fork out far more that the £45 charged for the suites if the Puri Tempo Doeloe was located at the beach. They are very tastefully decorated in the traditional Balinese style with many charming handicrafts. The complex includes a wellness area and yoga studio and the restaurant serves very tasty Balinese and French cuisine. This hotel is ideal for those who enjoy the good things in life.
191 E2/3
✉ Jl. Bypass Ngurah Rai 209
☎ 0361 28 65 42;
www.hotelpuritempodoeloe.com

Where to...
Eat and Drink

Prices
Expect to pay per person for a main course, excluding drinks and service:
£ under Rp60,000 **££** Rp60,000–120,000 **£££** over Rp120,000

JIMBARAN

Bawang Merah Beachfront Restaurant £–£££
Located a short distance away from the hustle and bustle of the seafood restaurants, but in pole position on the beach at Jimbaran, this restaurant is very popular after 5pm (reservations essential). Guests have more space than usual and the tables are pleasantly decorated. If you have something to celebrate you can reserve a Romantic Table, which comes with a bouquet of roses, champagne cocktail and other courtesies. The menu features not only fish and seafood but also several vegetarian and meat dishes. The real winner is the lobster platter that costs Rp400,000 including all the trimmings. If you spend a certain amount you will get a free transfer from the holiday resorts in the south.
190 C2 Kelan
0361 77 02 10;
www.jimbaranbeachrestaurant.com
Daily noon–10pm

KUTA

Batan Waru Kafe £–££
There is a wide range of delicious Balinese-Indonesian dishes on the menu, also making it popular with many Indonesian tourists. If you have difficulty choosing from among all the delicacies, you will not be disappointed if you decide on the *nasi campur batan*, the small *rijsttafel* here comes in two versions (Rp75,000 and Rp95,000).
190 C2 Lippo Mall, Kuta, Jl. Kartika Plaza
0361 897 80 74 Daily from 8am.

Chez Gado Gado £££
You can choose to dine outdoors under trees strung with lanterns, or by candlelight right on the beach, or in the palm-leaf restaurant, but no matter where you sit you will be delighted by the elegant ambience and the Mediterranean-French cuisine, which has the reputation of being the finest of its kind in Seminyak. The tapas platter (2 persons, Rp250,000) makes an excellent sunset snack and you can spoil yourself by ordering the appropriate wine to accompany it (from Rp450,000 a bottle).
190 C2 Jl. Camplung Tanduk (Beach Road) 99, Seminyak 0361 73 69 66;
www.gadogadorestaurant.com
Daily 8am–3pm and 5pm–10:30pm

Kopi Pot £–££
The "coffee pot" was founded in the early 1990s and it is the best place in town for coffee, cakes and pastries, as well as a popular venue for breakfasts and dinners. Sit outside under the shade of the trees on the terrace overlooking the street and enjoy Indonesian and Thai specialities. The seafood dishes are relatively reasonably priced.
190 C2
Jl. Legian (50m/160ft south of Hotel 101)
0361 75 26 14 Daily from 8am

Poppies Restaurant ££
This delightful restaurant is set in a breathtakingly beautiful garden and has been a culinary institution

in Kuta since 1973, and as it is very popular, reservations are essential. Insider Tip There isn't anywhere else in Kuta that has an atmosphere as romantic as Poppies and it is famed for its top-quality, sophisticated Balinese and international cuisine. Once you have eaten here, you will want to return time and time again. The house specialities – and far and away most expensive dishes on the menu – include the *rijsttafel* (2 persons, Rp259,000) and the Fisherman's Basket (2 persons, Rp395,000).

190 C2 Jl. Legian, Kuta, Poppies Lane I
0361 75 10 59; www.poppiesbali.com
Daily 8am–11pm

SANUR

Manik Organik Bali £

Organic food is rare in Bali – especially if it is vegetarian, vegan, or raw. The Manik Organik has filled this niche. You can sit outside in the garden, which is also a great opportunity to meet other friendly people. They have various courses (including yoga and meditation) on offer and Insider Tip a well-stocked shop with all kinds of ecological and organic products.

191 E2/3 Jl. Tamblingan 85
0361 8 55 33 80; www.manikorganikbali.com
Daily 8am–11pm

Three Monkeys

This restaurant's name is a tongue-in-cheek reference to its three founders. It enjoys cult status – as does its offshoot in Ubud. The fusion food skilfully combines Mediterranean and Balinese elements in a very creative fashion. The pizzas (also Turkish-style) are divine, and if greens are your thing, you are sure to find just what you are looking for from among the 17 different salads on the menu.

191 E2/3
Jl. Danau Tamblingan 0361 28 60 02; www.threemonkeyscafebali.com
Daily from 11am

Where to... Shop

Kuta is the epicentre of shopping in south Bali. This is also where dirt-cheap bootleg copies of CDs and DVDs are sold, but remember that you cannot take them through customs when you return home. Anyone caught with bootleg CDs and DVDs in their luggage will have to pay a hefty fine. The same applies to counterfeit goods carrying the labels of popular brands.

JIMBARAN

Jenggala Keramik

Jenggala showcases the most beautiful, top quality, aesthetically pleasing ceramics imaginable.

190 C2 Jl. Uluwatu II 0361 70 33 11; www.jenggala.com Daily 10am–8pm

KUTA

The thousands of shops make Kuta one large shopping centre and this means that you will probably not know where to go to first. Here are a few tips to make things a little easier for you:

Beachwalk Shopping Center

Some tourists spend a whole day window-shopping, shopping and eating in Bali's newest and most sophisticated shopping mall – you will either love it or hate it.

190 C2 Jl. Pantai Kuta
0361 8 46 48 88; www.beachwalkbali.com
Daily 10am–10pm

Discovery Shopping Mall

The largest shopping mall in Bali is filled with renowned international brand shops.

190 C2 Jl. Kartika Plaza 0361 75 55 22; www.discoveryshoppingmall.com
Daily 10am–10pm

Geneva Handicraft Center
Kuta is the only place where you can find a place like this, a shopping centre devoted exclusively to arts and crafts.
190 C2 Jl. Raya Kerobokan 100
0361 73 35 42; www.genevahandicraft.com
Daily 9am–8pm

Kuta Art Market
No matter what kind of handicraft is crafted on Bali, you will be able to find it here. The offer is as bewildering as it is large.
190 C2 Corner Jl. Bakung Sari and Jl. Kartika Plaza Daily 10am–10pm

Kuta Square
This multi-storey department store specialises in brand-name surf and sportswear.
190 C2
Corner Jl. Bakung Sari/Jl. Kartika Plaza
Daily 9am–10pm

SANUR

Rumah Fair Trade Indonesia
Bali's most eco-friendly shop offers a wide selection of Fair Trade products made by artisans from all over Indonesia. The range includes clothing, cosmetics, gifts and jewellery, as well as bags, instruments, home accessories, toys and organic food. It is a short way out of town but a taxi trip will only cost a few rupiahs.
191 E2/3
Ruko Griya Sanur, Jl. Bypass Ngurah Rai
0361 28 35 55 Daily 9am–6pm

NUSA DUA

Bali Collection
This shopping mall, which is actually more of a shopping village, is as expensive as everything else in this upscale resort. You will often pay one third of the price more here, for the same products.
191 D1 Bali Tourism Development Corporation (BTDC) Complex
0361 77 16 62; www.bali-collection.com
Daily 10am–10pm

Where to... Go Out

Kuta's nightlife scene is legendary, possibly even the hottest action in the southern hemisphere. However, you will not be aware of this in Jimbaran, and in Nusa Dua the only thing night owls can do is hang out in the hotel bars. And then there's Sanur where evening entertainment usually consists of unobtrusive live music. During the day, hundreds of businesses attempt to get a small slice of the large tourism cake. Pamphlets are displayed in all places of accommodation and for the most part you can usually also book on the spot; the price usually includes a free transfer.

KUTA

Bali Bungy
Adrenalin junkies can get their kicks in Kuta with a jump from a 45m (148ft) bungee tower. The gear is well maintained and the prices are hefty (US$100) and there is such a demand that that there is often a long wait before you can make the leap.
190 C2
J. Hackett Kuta, Double Six Club, Jl. Arjuna
03 6 51 73 04 66;
www.ajhacket.com

Bounty Discotheque
The Bounty Disco is a replica pirate ship with several bars, dance floors and snack shops. It is one of the top party places in Kuta. The atmosphere is relaxed, the music mainstream (often live), relatively high priced drinks.
190 C2 Jl. Legian
0361 75 66 66;
www.bountydiscotheque.com
Daily from 11am

Engine Room
Welcome to the machine! The Engine Room's interior is decked out with plenty of metal and every night the crowds dance to deafening house, hip-hop and R&B; lots of parties, no dress code.
190 C2 Jl. Legian 81 0361 75 51 88; www.engineroombali.com Daily 10pm–4am

Ku De Ta
The Ku De Ta lounge bar is *the* place to see and be seen in Seminyak. Head there in the late afternoon to make the day last longer, stay at the seaside, stretch out on one of the sun loungers, sip cool cocktails and catch a glimpse of the who's who in Seminyak. In spite of the absolutely exorbitant prices (beer from Rp50,000, cocktails from Rp150,000), it is packed from early in the morning until late at night.
190 C2 Jl. Kayu Aya 9 0361 73 69 69; www.kudeta.net Daily 10am–2am

Pro Surf
Pro Surf is representative of the dozens of surfing centres in Kuta. You can book a course (1 day from £40, 10 days from £340, 2 hours private coaching £85), rent boards, join a surf camp and find accommodation that is popular with surfers.
190 C2 Jl. Pantai Kuta 21 0361 75 12 00; www.prosurfschool.com

Sky Garden Lounge
Trendy, stylish lounge-disco-bar complex with fabulous views of Kuta. It has four floors where guests dance to house and hip-hop, there is also live music and an entertainment programme with fire-eaters and acrobats.
190 C2 Jl. Legian 61 0361 75 54 23; www.skygardenbali.com Daily 5pm–3am

Waterbom Park
With about a dozen slides, Kuta's water park is definitely one of the biggest in the southern hemisphere and – if you believe Tripadvisor – it is one of the three best worldwide.
190 C2 Jl. Kartika Plaza, Kuta 0361 75 56 76; www.waterbom-bali.com Daily 9am–6pm, Rp520,000

SANUR

Adora Super Club
If you miss Kuta's nightlife in Sanur, this club is for you. It can accommodate over 1,000 party guests and has live music and DJs every night; karaoke fans will also be happy here.
191 E2/3 Jl. Bypass Ngurah Rai 888 0361 784 03 88; www.adorabali.blogspot.com Daily 10pm–4am

Casablanca
Since its beginnings as a pub and dance floor restaurant in 2012, the Casablanca has been a hotspot in Sanur's nightlife. There is live music – blues, reggae, rock, pop – every evening, as well as entertainment nights several times a week. Decent prices for drinks.
191 E2/3 Jl. Danau Tamblingan 120 0361 28 72 63; www.casablancasanur.com Daily 10am–3am/4am

Jazz Bar and Grille
Pub-restaurant with live jazz (all styles from Dixieland to free jazz) and the jam sessions (Tue and Sat from 10pm) have earned it an excellent reputation.
191 E2/3 Jl. By Pass Ngurah Rai 15–16 0361 28 72 55 Daily 11am–2am

NUSA DUA

Wira Water Sports Bali
Water sports enthusiasts will find their mecca in Benoa, north of Nusa Dua. This is where you can parasail, water-ski, jet ski, go fly boarding (ca. £32) and wakeboarding, as well as other marine activities. You can book water sports packages that also include transfers.
191 D1 Tanjung Benoa 0812 36 15 82 43; www.water-sport-bali.com

The Centre

Little Treats

Just like Hitchcock's *The Birds*

See thousands of herons in the evening as they come home to roost in **Petulu** (➤ 77), but be sure to seek shelter from their droppings.

Colourful Flutter

You can see one of the world's largest butterflies at the **Bali Butterfly Park** (➤ 90), which is on the way to Pura Luhur Batukau.

Spiritual Ubud

To pamper your body and soul pay a visit to Bali Spirit (Jl. Raya Sukma; www.balispirit.com) in **Ubud** (➤ 74).

The Centre

Getting Your Bearings

The landscape here is stunningly beautiful in every direction you look. There are lush, emerald green terraced rice fields on gently rolling hills and steep mountain slopes. Glistening ponds and pools adorned with pink and white lotus blossoms, swaying palm groves that merge into magnificent, colourful gardens – and the entire area is presided over by the majestic cone of Gunung Agung.

The Bali featured in glossy magazines is truly a feast for the eyes – and you can enjoy it to the full here in the island's centre, while the cultural metropolis of Ubud provides an urban counterpoint to this natural glory. This is the island's cultural and artistic heartbeat, it was discovered by European and American artists in the 1930s and they established it as an artist's enclave. Today tourism in Ubud has commercialized art and culture and there is nowhere else on Bali that has such a high a concentration of studios, artisan workshops, museums and art galleries. Every evening colourful, traditional dance performances are performed on numerous stages throughout the town. The sound of the gamelan can always be heard somewhere in the background and there is no shortage of festivals and religious ceremonies – nor of temples, shrines and traditional villages. And since the whole of the island centre offers dozens of walks, hikes and bicycle tours, the region is also a real treat for active holidaymakers.

Cycling in the central region of Bali may be physically demanding but it offers breathtaking views as a reward

TOP 10

Don't Miss

At Your Leisure

The oversized demon that guards the entrance to the Goa Gajah (➤ 91) is a popular subject for photos

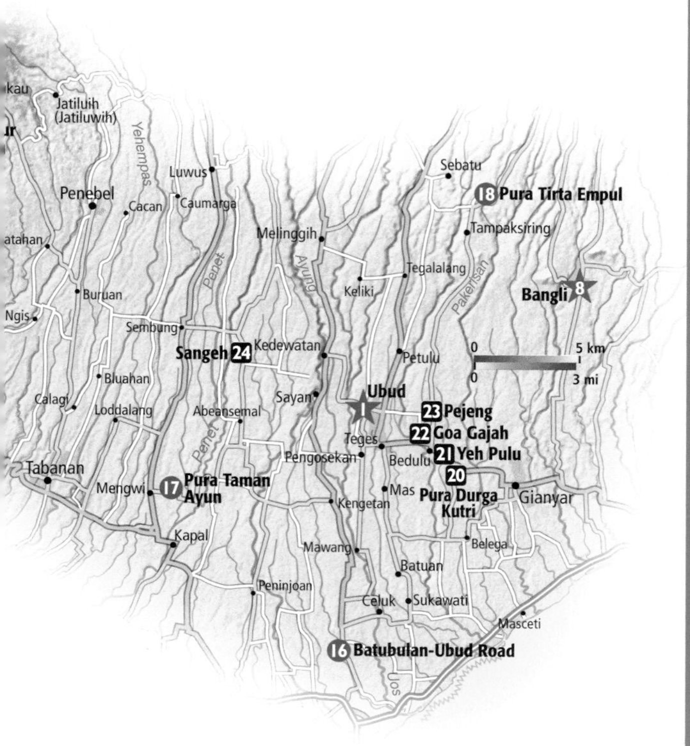

The Centre

Four Perfect Days

The leitmotif of central Bali is of course its rich culture but this itinerary also takes in numerous breathtaking nature spots. A rental car is absolutely essential and Ubud is the ideal base – at least for the first three days.

Day 1

Morning

You need to set out early (at around 7am) because of the heavy traffic on the 16 **Batubulan-Ubud Road** (➤ 83) and you need to be in **Batubulan** (➤ 83) before 9am for the Barong dance drama, which is well worth seeing. At about 10:30am you should continue on to the **Bali Bird Park** (➤ 84) and the **Bali Reptile Park** (➤ 84) in Singapadu, before taking the road to 1 **Ubud** (➤ 74) via **Celuk** (➤ 84), **Sukawati** (➤ 85) and **Batuan** (➤ 85). This route is lined with workshops and artisans.

Afternoon

After all the sightseeing, and maybe even some shopping, it is a good idea to take it easy with just a visit to the **Monkey Forest** (➤ 76).

Evening

Now it is time to see one of the excellent traditional dance performances held every night at 7:30pm in **Puri Saren** (➤ 97).

Day 2

Morning/Afternoon

You should devote the entire morning and afternoon to the **Jl. Raya Ubud** (➤ 75) – preferably on foot or by bicycle.

Afternoon

Make sure to finish your sightseeing by 4pm at the latest so that you have enough time to take a taxi to nearby **Tegallalang** (➤ 77) to see the rice terraces; after about an hour, you can continue on to **Petulu** (➤ 77).

Evening

The **Agung Rai Museum of Art** (➤ 76; right) is the best place in Ubud for an exquisite evening meal followed by a Legong performance.

Day 3

Morning

To avoid the masses of tourists at the ⑱ **Pura Tirta Empul** and **Gunung Kawi** (➤ 88) shrines, you will have to make another early start. Aim to get to the first destination, Gunung Kawi, at 8–9am; the next stop is the Pura Tirta Empul and then a detour via ㉓ **Pejeng** (➤ 92) to ★8 **Bangli** (➤ 80)

Afternoon

You will now have plenty of time to visit the **Pura Kehen** (➤ 80), as well as the **Desa Tradisional Pengelipuran** (➤ 82) before heading on to the ⑳ **Pura Durga Kutri** (➤ 91), the rock reliefs in ㉑ **Yeh Pulu** (➤ 91) and the ㉒ **Goa Gajah** (➤ 91) and back to Ubud.

Evening

Balinese culture is all well and good but maybe not every night. A pleasant change could be a romantic dinner in **Murni's Warung** (➤ 95) followed by jazz and tropical cocktails at the **Laughing Buddha** (➤ 97).

Day 4

Morning

On your way to Mengwi, it is a good idea to make a detour (12km/7.5mi there and back) to visit the monkey forest at ㉔ **Sangeh** (➤ 92). You should not spend too much time there, as you need to be at the ⑰ **Pura Taman Ayun** (➤ 86) before 10am in order to beat the crowds that arrive later and to set out on the scenic route to Gunung Batukau.

Afternoon

You will probably want to spend at least an hour at the ⑲ **Pura Luhur Batukau** (➤ 89) and you will then have no trouble at all spending the rest of the day looking at the scenic rice terraces of **Jati Luwih** (➤ 89). Not a bad idea since you can then spend the night in one of the incomparably beautiful **Soka Jati Luwil Villas** (➤ 93).

Ubud

Artists from Europe and America searching for their Shangri-La discovered Bali in the 1920s. Ubud, which was already the cultural and artistic heart of the island at the time, was still in a pristine state and – from the travel reports by the early visitors – must have come very close to our idea of the Garden of Eden. Ubud attracted flower children and backpackers in the 1960s and 1970s and then came the tourists, first individuals and then en mass. And today? Today, the once idyllic village has become the second-largest tourist centre on the island, after Kuta.

Once known as a place of healing (Ubud means "medicine") it is hard to believe that this town only has a population of 30,000 inhabitants as constant traffic congests the main street, which is lined with an endless row of shops and boutiques, cafés, restaurants, pubs and galleries. The never-ending traffic jams of the rush "hour" last from 10am to 5pm. And the accommodation options become more expensive, cooler and more exclusive with every year.

Ubud's most recent boom came in 2010 with the release of the Hollywood film *Eat Pray Love*. In the film adaptation of the autobiographical novel by Elizabeth Gilbert, Julia Roberts – alias Liz – arrives in Ubud and finds herself and love. Since then, whole battalions of female tourists have made their way to Ubud in search of peace of mind and the number of yoga, meditation and treatment centres, as well as spas and wellness hotels, has skyrocketed.

Altar offerings in the Puri Saren Palace

In the main street of Ubud countless shops vie for customers

That is one side of the coin, but on the flip side, there is nowhere else in Bali – and possibly in Indonesia or even all of Southeast Asia – like Ubud when it comes to art, culture and spirituality. The small town is nestled in the midst of magnificent natural and cultural landscapes and there are countless attractions waiting to be discovered, along with many hikes and pleasant walks. This is reason enough for many visitors to choose Ubud as the base for their holiday in Bali; especially those who do not want to spend most of the time (sun) bathing.

Insider Tip

Jl. Raya Ubud

Most of the sights in Ubud are located along the main road, the Jl. Raya Ubud, which runs all the way through the centre of town. These include the royal palace, the **Puri Saren**, which is built in the traditional style of architecture and is situated opposite the immense covered market. It is worth visiting during the day, especially on Saturday afternoon when girls practice the Legong dance in the grounds, and every evening when the residence provides the atmospheric setting for **Balinese dance drama** (► 28) performances.

The **Puri Lukisan**, know as the "Palace of Paintings" is just a few steps away to the west. The museum was established in 1956 by the then King of Ubud and the Dutch painter Rudolf Bonnet, it was the island's first private museum and houses the most important collection of Balinese art. You should make sure that you have enough time to explore the three main buildings with their mid-20th century art, contemporary works and paintings by Bonnet and other foreign artists.

A mere 500m (1,600ft) further on, is the **Blanco Renaissance Museum** with art – sometimes similar in style to Dalí – by **Don Antonio Blanco** who was born in the Philippines but initially lived and worked in the USA. Throughout his life, he was his own favourite subject.

The rice terraces in Tegallalang are a sea of different shades of green

From here, the road continues as Jl. Raya Campuan uphill to the suburb of Campuan where the German artist Walter Spies lived in 1927. Together with the Prince of Ubud and his fellow artist Bonnet, he founded the **Pita Maha** artists' association in 1936 with the aim of invigorating Balinese painting through European traditions. It has since become the nucleus of the colony of artists in Ubud. And, the works captured on canvas in Bali since its founding days are presented in an exemplary fashion in the **Neka Art Museum**, which was opened in several palace-like buildings in 1982. The museum is arranged thematically and many art connoisseurs find it even better than the (larger) Puri Lukisan (➤ 75).

Other Highlights

If you want something more down-to-earth after all the Ubud art, you should turn off Jl. Raya Ubud into Jl. Wanara Wana, which is better known as Monkey Forest Road. Walk along for about 10 minutes until the shop zone ends at a forest with gigantic moss-covered banyan trees and overgrown shrines, which appear to have come straight out of a fairy tale. This is part of the **Monkey Forest**, home to around 300 long-tailed macaques. The Balinese consider them (and the entire forest) sacred but their status doesn't stop them from being very cheeky – or maybe that is why they behave so badly, simply because they know they can get away with it. They steal whatever they can get their hands on from those visiting the forest – their preferred items include cameras, keys, glasses and even bags and backpacks. Insider Tip So do take heed of the signs that warn against touching or feeding them.

If you feel like rounding off the day with a little more culture then head to the **Agung Rai Museum of Art** (ARMA) in the southern suburb of Pengosekan. The private collection belonging to the most important collector of Balinese art was opened as a museum, and meeting place for artists, in 1996. It houses an exceptional collection of Bali artworks by iconic local and foreign artists, including art by Walter Spies, Rudolf Bonnet and other renowned European artists. The knowledgeable guides offer very informative tours of the collection. The ARMA is also the best place in Bali for cultural workshops. No matter whether you want to study painting or carving, dancing or cooking – everything is available here. The complex also has an open-air stage where dance dramas – usually the Legong – are performed every evening. Alternatively, you can enjoy a traditional Balinese buffet meal.

Herons and Rice Terraces

About 4km (2.5mi) north of Ubud, on Jl. Raya Petulu in the direction of Penelokan, is the small village **Petulu**. Every evening at around 6pm, just in time for sunset, the sky above the village darkens with swarms of white herons returning to roost in the the trees and fields. It is a real spectacle as the air seethes with masses of birds and droppings rain down from the sky. You should find shelter if you don't want to make the journey home spattered and smelly, fortunately, there are plenty of places where you can find protection. Insider Tip

North of Petulu, on the road to Penelokan, is the village of **Tegallalang,** which is responsible for the fact that Bali's rice terraces, in their entirety, are now a UNESCO World Heritage Site. The best time to visit the "steps of the gods" (➤ 77), as the Balinese call them, is late in the afternoon (or early in the morning), when the rays of the setting sun illuminates the terraces. There are many restaurants with balconies offering panoramic views, where you will not only enjoy the scenery, but also have a respite from all the annoying souvenir vendors. Insider Tip

Even though the long-tailed macaques look cute, they are not to be trifled with

TAKING A BREAK

On your Ubud sightseeing trip you will have no trouble finding places for refreshment breaks – there are hundreds of bistros, cafés and restaurants everywhere you go. If you are looking for something special, **Clear** (➤ 95) near the Puri Lukisan is a good choice for snacks or lunch, coffee and cake, or dinner.

191 E4

Tourist Office Yayasan Bina Wisata
Jl. Raya Ubud 0361 97 32 85 Daily 8am–8pm

Perama Tour & Travel
Jl. Hanuman 0361 97 33 16; www.peramatour.com

Puri Lukisan
Jl. Raya Ubud 0361 97 11 59; www.museumpurilukisan.com
Daily 9am–6pm Rp50,000

Blanco Renaissance Museum
Jl. Raya Campuan 0361 97 55 02; www.blancomuseum.com
Daily 9am–5pm Rp80,000

Neka Art Museum
Raya Campuan 0361 2 97 50 74; www.museumneka.com
Mon–Sat 9am–5pm, Sun from noon Rp50,000, children free

Monkey Forest
Monkey Forest Road; www.monkeyforestubud.com 8:30–6 Rp40,000

Botanic Garden
Jl. Tirta Tawar 0361 97 09 51 Daily 9am–5pm Rp50,000

Agung Rai Museum of Art
Jl. Raya Pengosekan Ubud 0361 97 66 59; www.armabali.com
Daily 9am–6pm Rp50,000

With a little luck, you may get to see one of the most colourful Hindu ceremonies while in Ubud

INSIDER INFO

- Practical information about Ubud is available in the **online magazine** at www.ubud community.com.
- The best way to explore the city is by **bicycle**; you will find bicycle and moped rentals on almost every corner in Ubud.
- The tourist office and many shops sell the **Bali Pathfinder** hiking map, which has descriptions of the numerous hikes and cycle paths in the countryside around Ubud. Free town **maps** are available in all places of accommodation, as well as the tourist information office.
- If you want to pamper your body and soul in Ubud, the holistic range offered by **Bali Spirit** (Jl. Raya Sukma; tel: 0361 9 08 01 22; www.balispirit.com) is recommended.
- At the **Elephant Safari Park** near Tegallalang, you can come in close contact with the elephants during the shows or on a trekking tour. Bookings can be made through **Bali Adventure Tours** (tel: 0361 72 14 80; www.baliadventuretours.com).
- Wherever there are many tourists, there is usually also crime. If anything is stolen, you should contact the police station in the city centre (Jl. Raya Ubud; tel: 0361 97 53 16).
- Moped accidents involving tourists are sometimes a daily occurrence in Ubud. The **Ubud Clinic's** emergency service (Jl. Raya Campuan 36; tel: 0361 97 49 11; www.ubudclinic.baliklik.com) is open 24 hours a day.

Bangli

This former royal town lies at an altitude of 500m (1,600ft) and delights visitors with its pleasantly cool climate, a market held every three days and two sightseeing attractions, which are a must for those interested in culture.

Pura Kehen

This royal temple, which was probably built in the 13th century, is not only beautifully situated but it is also one of three holiest on the island. The complex is about 2km (1.2mi) north of the centre of Bangli, a little way off the main road towards Penelokan/Kintamani, and is located on a series of terraces on a gently sloping hillside lush with greenery.

Numerous stone guardian figures flank the grounds of the Pura Kehen

You will feel the special atmosphere as soon as you arrive at the car park – children with flowers in their hair show visitors the way while groups of festively dressed faithful with colourful towers of offerings prepare to enter the temple. Climb the **steep staircase** leading up to the temple and you will soon find yourself face to face with the gigantic, grim-faced **guardian figures** that flank the portal, which is richly decorated with reliefs and arabesques. This leads through to the first of **seven terraces**; the top one is dominated by an 11-tiered ***meru*** (pagoda) dedicated to Shiva.

The Sacred Banyan

Everywhere you look, the Balinese are busying themselves with flowers and fruits that are presented as offerings to the gods. Clouds of incense hang heavily in the air in the temple courtyards, all of which are enclosed with moss-covered walls and adorned with shrines. However, all of this work created by human hands seems trivial when you see the **outer courtyard,** which is entirely in the shade of what is possibly the largest and most revered tree in Bali. The banyan tree (from the fig family) is immediately recognisable by its network of thousands of aerial roots that form the trunk, which has an estimated diameter of 15m (50ft). In the face of this colossus, you will immediately understand why banyan trees, which provide shade in most village squares on the island, are considered sacred by the Balinese.

Pengelipuran

There is also one such banyan in Pengelipuran, a village 4km (2.5mi) north of the Pura Kehen on the left-hand side of the road leading to Lake Batur. You will see the *desa tradisional* (traditional village) signpost. The main path through the **village** (➤ 16) is laid out along an imaginary sea-mountain axis; it is a paved promenade lined with well tended flowerbeds behind which are moss-covered walls that separate the individual family homesteads. These walls are not intended to cut them off from curious neighbours but to protect them from *butas*, the demons that are always eager to make life miserable. The **small offerings** in front of the entrances to the farms are there to ward off these evil spirits.

Beyond each gate is a courtyard surrounded by buildings, the buildings are not arranged randomly but are aligned with the **cosmic system**, and each building has a pre-determined place. Even the architectural dimensions of the complex follow strict rules based on the physical measurements of the head of the family.

TAKING A BREAK

Midori Warung (Jl. Merdeka 108B) is on the southern outskirts of Bangli, on the road from Pura Kehen through the village. The charming wooden pavilions on stilts seem to hover above frog ponds. As is customary in Bali, you sit on cushions on the floor (although there are also tables) and enjoy unpretentious, but really delicious, Balinese dishes. The specialities include Mujair fish – fried (*goreng*) or steamed (*nyat nyat*) – served with rice, sambal and small pieces of cucumber and shallots.

---

191 F5

Bangli Government Tourism Office
Jl. Brigjen Ngurah Rai
03 61 9 15 37

Desa Tradisional Pengelipuran
Daily 8am–6pm Rp15,000

Pura Kehen
Jl. Sriwijaya
Daily 9am–5pm Rp15,000

The village of Pengelipuran is laid out according to traditional Balinese laws

INSIDER INFO

Most visitors to Bali make their holiday base in the south of the island but it is easy to go on **day excursions** to see central Bali's highlights. You can either rent a car (with or without a driver, ➤ 33) or join an organised tour. There are more than enough tour operators to choose from but **Perama Tours** (tel: 0361 75 08 08; www.peramatour.com) has branches in all of the tourist centres and has been in business for decades. They offer tours, for example, that start in the south of the island and proceed along the "road of artisans" to Ubud; another itinerary takes in the major sights around Ubud, Bangli and Mengwi. The prices are around Rp400,000 per person and the tours include all admission fees, lunch and – importantly – an expert, English-speaking guide.  The tours go ahead even when there are only two participants meaning that they are almost always private, without the usual shopping fun and games you have to put up with on other organised bus tours.

16 Batubulan–Ubud Road

When you leave the holiday centres in the south and make your way into the centre of the island, you will have to endure the worst traffic in Bali, as this is the island's most densely populated area. Once you leave Denpasar and the last suburbs recede, you will heave a sigh of relief but then you plunge straight into the hustle and bustle of the "road of artisans" which begins in the village of Batubulan and ends in Ubud.

This route runs for around 30km (18mi) through numerous villages with hundreds – if not thousands – of small workshops where silversmiths, woodcarvers, stonemasons, and puppet makers churn out goods like assembly line workers. Almost everything here revolves around shopping, but it is also fine just to window-shop.

Batubulan

The first village along this route (with a rather unimpressive landscape) is lined with outlets selling stone sculptures of gods and demons, Buddhas, temple guards, mythological creatures, as well as modern motifs. Batubulan, which has almost merged with Denpasar, is the most important **centre of stone sculpting** on Bali. The main road – always busy with traffic – is one long display of sculptures. At the northern end of the village, the **Pura Puseh** temple is the best example of the skill and craftsmanship of the stonemasons. Its portal – believed to be the most richly decorated in all of Bali – is covered with reliefs, arabesques and other stone ornaments.

The stonemasons in Batubulan carve religious and mythological figures

An exotic hornbill in the Bali Bird Park

Singapadu

If you continue further along the main road through Batubulan, you will soon reach the turnoff to the neighbouring village of Singapadu, which boasts three animal parks in its immediate vicinity. In the 2ha (5 acres) of the **Bali Bird Park** there are over 1,000 birds in more than 250 different species – some fly free while others are kept in an enormous aviary. It is undoubtedly one of the loveliest bird parks in the entire Indonesian archipelago.

The admission fee is a bit steep (nearly £25) but it also includes entrance to the neighbouring **Bali Reptile Park** where 180 reptiles of 20 different species are housed in very cramped cages. You can also see the famous Komodo dragons, crocodiles, giant turtles, huge snakes and all the other animals that creep and crawl in Indonesia.

On the way towards Celuk (► below) you reach the **Bali Zoo** where – as is so often the case – animals from all around the world endure a rather sad existence. If you find the zoo too upsetting, you can lighten the mood by spending some time in the adjacent **treetop adventure park**, where you can swing through the trees just like Tarzan.

Celuk

The stronghold of **Balinese jewellery** production grows more glamorous every year; the elegant shops (that seem to be able to swallow up whole busloads of visitors) keep expanding and also demand increasingly absurd dollar prices for their goods. Anybody who buys items here has only himself or herself to blame. Insider Tip Instead, you should head for the small workshops away from the main streets, where you can watch the artisans at work and buy their goods at significantly lower prices. It is also possible to have jewellery made to your own designs.

Sukawati

The next stop is firmly in the hands of the weavers who make **baskets and ceremonial umbrellas** – and they are incredibly skilful. In addition, Sukawati is famous throughout the island for the shadow-puppets produced here. There is also a wide range of other arts and crafts offered in Sukawati, all of which are available under one roof at the **Pasar Seni** (daily 7am–7pm) art market. Thousands of tourists are hustled through the building every day, the prices are high and there is little chance to bargain.

Batuan

Together with the village of **Mas**, a little further along the road to Ubud, Batuan is regarded as Bali's **wood carving** centre. Pieces of furniture are opulently decorated with carvings and masks and statues are also produced in every size. It is also famous as an art colony and there are numerous galleries exhibiting traditional Balinese paintings.

TAKING A BREAK

The hotter the weather, the better spicy food tastes. But there are many grades of spiciness, as you will soon discover in the **Special Sambal** on the main road in Sukawati (Jl. Raya Batu Bulan). This restaurant attracts more locals than tourists and you will be able to try out around 20 different chilli pastes along with the normal Balinese fare. Try to eat your meal with your fingers (the right hand only!) just as the local Balinese do. The fresh fruit juices are also very tasty. Everything is dirt cheap – drinks cost ca. Rp6,000 and meals about Rp30,000.

---

191 D/E3/4

Bali Bird Park & Bali Reptile Park

191 D3 Jl. Serma Cok Ngurah Gambir, Singapadu
0361 29 93 52; www.bali-bird-park.com
Daily 9am–5:30pm
Rp430,000 (20% discount for early online bookings)

Bali Zoo

191 D3 Jl. Raya Singapadu, Singapadu
0361 29 43 57; www.bali-zoo.com
Daily 9am–6pm, Wed and Sat also 6pm–9:30pm
Rp378,000 (there are also package deals incl. transport, animal shows and safaris)

INSIDER INFO

Another aspect of Batubulan's artistic side is the **dance dramas** (➤ 28), which are performed on several stages near the village temples. They are extremely colourful and very photogenic. The Barong is staged from 9am and the Legong and other plays attract many visitors in the evening from 6pm.

17 Pura Taman Ayun

Temples are as much a part of Bali as gods and demons. If you are interested in the vibrant culture of the island then you must visit the "temple of the floating garden". It is the main attraction in Mengwi, Bali's second-largest temple after the Pura Besakih and, above all, it is absolutely beautiful.

It is hard to believe that the rather lively – but also rather nondescript – large village of **Mengwi** was once the seat of one of the most powerful kingdoms on Bali. That was just over 120 years ago. The Pura Taman Ayun is the most important architectural testimony to the royal dynasty that ruled Mengwi for several centuries.

The temple was built in 1634 and extensively renovated in 1937, and its countless tall *merus* make it easy to see from afar. But it is only when you are up close that you fully

INSIDER INFO

A footbridge leads into the sanctuary of the Pura Taman Ayun but – as is the case with all temples on Bali – foreign visitors are only permitted to enter the first two temple courtyards but not the third one, which is the most sacred. However, you are allowed to look at it and for the best **view over the whole complex** you should climb up the *Kulkul* drum tower, which is located on left corner of the second temple courtyard. Insider Tip

understand why it the name means "temple of the floating garden" or "garden temple in water". The temple is on a **man-made island** with a waist-high wall and surrounded by a moat filled with lotus blossoms and water lilies. Looking from the outside, the temple appears to float on water. However, the moat was created mainly to demarcate the complex from all things worldly. And – according to the myths – it was done this way because the gods like to bathe in the water when they are present at temple festivities.

Pura Taman Ayun temple is a lush tropical idyll

The temple is surrounded by a charming **tropical garden** with lots of flowering shrubs, fruit and frangipani trees, as well as spectacularly coloured flowers, that create a wonderful setting for photographs of the temple. There are paths that wind their way through the grounds to many picnic areas.

TAKING A BREAK

The picnic pavilions in the gardens outside of the temple are perfect places for taking a short break. You can buy some inexpensive fresh fruit and snacks at the market stalls opposite the temple. If you aren't keen on a picnic but still want to enjoy the view, then head for the **Water Garden Restaurant** (daily from 9am) opposite the temple.

---

191 D4 Daily 8am–6pm Rp20,000

18 Pura Tirta Empul

North of Ubud the land gently rises upwards to the belt of mountains in the centre. The landscape is characterised by swathes of rolling rice terraces dotted with small, traditional villages, sacred shrines and temple complexes, one of which is Pura Tirta Empul.

If you follow the road past **Petulu** (➤ 77) and **Tegallalang** (➤ 77), you will soon arrive at the woodcarvers' village of Pujung. From here it is only a short distance the hamlet of Tampaksiring with the nearby **holy spring shrine**, Tirta Empul. It is believed that the spring was created by the god Indra himself, and it has been one of the most popular pilgrimage destinations in Bali for over 1,000 years.

Today, the faithful still believe in the magical healing powers of a dip in the cool waters that gush out of waterspouts into the **stone swimming pools**. The bulky structure above the temple was once the summer palace of the former President Sukarno.

Bathing in the holy water is certainly refreshing

TAKING A BREAK

There are numerous **food stalls** and small restaurants in front of the temple complexes of Tirta Empul and Gunung Kawi (➤ box), that serve simple – but absolutely authentic – Balinese dishes.

---

188 A2

Pura Tirta Empul
Daily 8am–6pm
Rp20,000

INSIDER INFO

The megalithic rock monuments of the royal tombs at **Gunung Kawi** (which means the "mountain of poetry", daily 8am–6pm; www.penaka.com, admission Rp20,000) were carved into the black volcanic rock about 1,000 years ago. The approach is through ancient rice terraces that lead to a picturesque canyon. Whether or not they are tombs is uncertain, quite a few archaeologists believe them to be memorials to deified rulers. Whatever the case may be, the site certainly has a special, almost magical atmosphere – especially in the soft light of the early morning.

19 Pura Luhur Batukau

The mountain temple of Pura Luhur Batukau, which is surrounded by verdant forest and often shrouded in mist, has the most magical aura of all of Bali's temples. The nearby Jati Luwih rice terraces are among the most beautiful in Asia and have been designated a UNESCO World Heritage Site.

Dating back to the 11th century, the Pura Luhur Batukau temple lies at an altitude of 817m (2,680ft) on the south-east slope of the 2,276m (7,467ft) Gunung Batukau (also: Batukaru) volcano. Although it is not one of the largest or most magnificent on the island, it is definitely one of the most important of the six Balinese national shrines. It is dedicated to **Mahadewa**, god of the Batukau mountain, whose shrine – a seven-tiered *meru* – rises up in the middle of a small spring-fed pond. The pond and spring are both sacred: shortly after Nyepi (➤ 18), the festival that celebrates the Balinese New Year, thousands of devout Balinese make a pilgrimage to this shrine to perform ritual purification ceremonies that last several days. The majority of the temple complex is closed to tourists during that time.

The real appeal of Pura Luhur Batukau is its location in the midst of a lush jungle landscape

Jati Luwih

"Simply beautiful" – the translation of the name Jati Luwih says it all. The "steps of the gods" or "stairs to heaven", as the Balinese – with their fine feeling for language – call the landscape of their rice terraces. Those nestled on the

slopes around the small village of Jati Luwih are amongst the most beautiful on Bali and were designated a UNESCO World Heritage Site in 2012. That speaks for itself and more than compensates for the few – but very winding – kilometres you will have to drive from the Batukau temple to the village.

The rice terraces of Jati Luwih are irrigated by the sophisticated *subak* system

TAKING A BREAK

All of Jati Luwih participates in rice terrace tourism. Along the scenic road through the terraces there are numerous restaurants where you can stop for refreshments. The one with perhaps the best view – but certainly very good *pisang goreng*, fried bananas – is **Warung Dhea** (tel: 0813 53 30 23 72; www.dheajatiluwih.com; daily from 7am).

187 D2 Daily 8am–6pm Rp15,000

INSIDER INFO

- A **notice board** at the temple states that those who still have their milk teeth, who are insane, are pregnant or the mother of small children who are still waiting to get their milk teeth, are all not allowed to enter the temple.
- On the road to Pura Luhur Batukau is the **Bali Butterfly Park** (187 D1; www.balibutterflypark.com; daily 8am–4:30pm, admission Rp85,000), the largest park of its kind in Southeast Asia. A net spans an area of 3,500m² (37,500ft²) allowing the delicate little creatures to flutter around in freedom. One of the insects in the park is the Atlas moth, one of the largest moths on earth, with a wingspan of up to 30cm (12in).
- The road from the Batukau temple to Jati Luwih is a **toll road** with a fee of Rp15,000 per person and Rp6,000 per vehicle. You must ask for a receipt and keep it on you in order to avoid being charged again on your return or onward journey (the toll points are located on both sides of the route).

At Your Leisure

20 Pura Durga Kutri

Tourists who visit the village of Kutri do so because of the Pura Durga Kutri (also: Pura Bukit Dharma) temple complex. This "sacred hill temple" is Bali's **most important shrine to Durga**, the goddess of death. She is considered to be the cruelest and most terrifying deity in the Balinese pantheon and is usually depicted as a ten-armed, clawed, man-eating monster. However, what makes the temple so fascinating is not so much the stone statue of the goddess (believed to be around 1,000 years old) but the very special, almost tangible, mystical atmosphere surrounding the sacred temple. And, there is also the panoramic view of the rice fields, hills and mountains. The best place to enjoy these to the full is at the top of the 99 steps of the staircase on the right-hand side of the temple. The stairs lead upwards through a gloomy rocky landscape and then beneath the gigantic crown of a banyan tree.

191 E4
Daily 9am–6pm Rp20,000

21 Yeh Pulu

The rock reliefs of Yeh Pulu, near the village of Bedulu, are well worth a visit. They were rediscovered in 1925 but the meaning of the 27m (88ft) long and 2m (6.5ft) high **band of reliefs** remains a mystery to this day. Most of the scenes depict everyday life and it seems that the scene unfolds from the left to right. One theory is that the relief depicts events from the life of the Hindu god Krishna.

191 E4
Daily 8am–6pm
Rp20,000

22 Goa Gajah

Shortly before Ubud, on the banks of Petanu River, is the Goa Gajah cave (image ➤ 71). It was only rediscovered in 1923 and is one of the most **important cultural monuments of the pre-Hindu era** on Bali. According to legend, the demon was carved into the rock sometime in the early 11th century. The mouth of the gigantic demonic face is the entrance and it is probably one of the most-photographed subjects on Bali. The cavern's T-shaped interior, which is around 13m (43ft) wide, is not especially interesting; it only contains the

A comic strip chiselled in stone – the Yeh Pulu rock reliefs

The long-tailed macaques are considered descendants of the monkey king Hanuman in the Indian epic *Ramayana* – their fame has gone to their heads, that has to be why they are so cheeky

remains of a phallus symbol along with a sculpture of the elephant god Ganesha.

191 E4

Daily 8am–6pm Rp20,000

23 Pejeng

The village of Pejeng was the seat of a kingdom between the 10th and 14th centuries. The state temple, **Pura Penataran Sasih,** dates from this period. The temple also houses a huge drum known as the Moon of Pejeng. With a diameter of around 1.60m (5.3ft), it is the largest prehistoric bronze gong in the world. It is thought to have been produced in a single casting in the 4th century BC and is elaborately decorated with stylised human heads (unfortunately, it is difficult to make them out as the gong's position is less than ideal).

191 E4

Daily 9am–5pm Rp20,000

24 Sangeh

There is only one monkey forest in Bali that is more famous than the one in Ubud (➤ 76) and that is the Sangeh **Monkey Forest**, a few kilometres west of Ubud on the northern edge of the village of Sangeh. In both cases the long-tailed macaques are sacred – and very cheeky. The forest trees – all nutmegs – are also sacred and soar upwards to heights of 40m (130ft) forming a dense, green canopy that only allows diffuse sunlight to penetrate. The forest itself would be a highlight, even without the monkeys, especially as it would then be possible to enjoy the experience without being accosted by brazen monkeys. Be very careful that the impudent monkeys do not make off with your camera or other items. They are especially annoying around the **Pura Bukit Sari** meditation temple. The temple is in the heart of this enchanted forest and its walls are overgrown with moss and lichen.

191 D5

Daily 8am–6pm Rp20,000

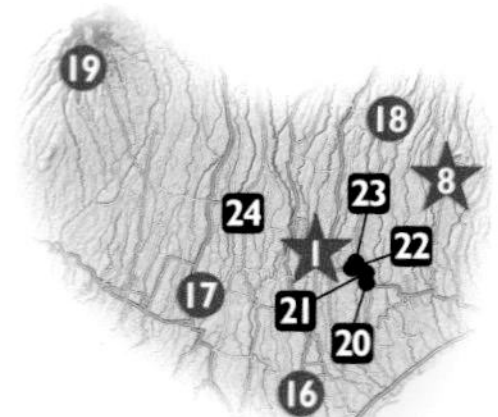

Where to... Stay?

Prices
Expect to pay per double room per night:
£ under Rp750,000 **££** Rp750,000–1.5 million **£££** over Rp1.5 million

Ubud is the tourist hub of central Bali and there is often a shortage of accommodation in July and August and at the end of the year – despite the wide selection on offer – as there are only a limited number of places to stay elsewhere in the centre. Jati Luwih is the exception and spending a night here, in the midst of one of the world's most scenic rice terraces, and seeing it in all of its many shades of green is certainly one of the best experiences of any trip to Bali. And, it is definitely quieter than Ubud.

JATI LUWIH

Batukaru Hotel £–£££

The rooms, bungalows and restaurant of the Batukaru Hotel are modern and very comfortable. There is a good-sized pool and organised tours are also available. The best views of the rice terraces are from the villas (officially ca. US$80 but £25 via a bookings website).

187 D2 Penebel
03 61 8 73 04 72;
www.batukaruhotel.com

Soka Jati Luwil Villas £–£££

Insider Tip This accommodation offers the best view of the Jati Luwih rice terraces. If you can arrange it, you should spend at least one night in one of the resort's comfortable bungalows. All of which are are built in the traditional rice barn style. There is also a small natural pool and restaurant, you can book tours (one option is a quad or ATV) and also rent bicycles. The official rack rate of US$108 for two persons is rather steep but you may find discounts of up to 60% if you use an internet booking website.

187 D2
On Jati Luwih, reservations through Bali Nature Land Tour Office, Jl. Raya Bypass Tanah Lot
0361 7 47 74 34;
www.balinatureland.com

UBUD

Bliss Ubud Bungalows ££

This property just outside of Ubud (free transfer) is set in the midst of a tropical garden and is surrounded by rice fields. It has been decorated with great attention to detail; the rooms are romantic (four-poster beds), without sacrificing modern amenities, and offer wonderful views. There is a large outdoor pool and spa section that is ideal for relaxation. And, this is all available for less than £45 a night. Those planning on an extended stay can rent fully furnished houses for around £350 a month.

191 E4 Jl. Raya Sanggingan, Lungsiakan
0361 97 92 72;
www.blissubudbungalow.com

Hotel Tjampuhan £££

Positioned on the edge of a deep valley, this hotel is absolutely captivating. There are breathtaking views from the restaurant and pool and all the amenities are top quality, including the spa (with Jacuzzi and artificial grotto),

and the exceptionally large wood-panelled rooms, which are furnished in the classic Balinese style. If you are able to afford ca. £85 a night for a room with breakfast, then this is where you should chose to do so.
191 E4 ✉ Jl. Tjampuhan
☎ 0361 97 53 68; www.tjampuhan-bali.com

Manyi Village ££–£££

Insider Tip

The resorts two-storey stone bungalows are an ideal place to enjoy your holiday idyll to the fullest. Here you can lie in bed (or in the bathtub) and look out over nothing but rice fields and enjoy absolute silence, broken only by the croaking of frogs and the quacking of the ducks. Everything here is of a high standard: the service, spa/wellness area and the pool. It comes as no surprise that most of the people staying here are repeat guests. The hotel is about a 10-minute drive from Ubud and there is a free shuttle service hourly between 8am and 10pm. The rack rate for a bungalow is around US$150 for two (incl. breakfast) but if you reserve through a booking website, you will pay about half the price.
191 E4 ✉ Banjar Laplapan ☎ 0361 8 98 78 98; www.manyivillageubud.com

Nick's Pension Hotel £–££

This guesthouse is idyllic and peaceful but it is also only a few minutes' walk away from the centre of town. The complex overlooks the rice terraces and offers simple guest rooms (from £13, with fan), some very tasteful rooms done in the Balinese style (£25–45, with air conditioning), as well as several detached cottages. There is also a swimming pool, a small spa, car rentals and organised tours.
191 E4 ✉ Jl. Bisma
☎ 0361 97 56 36;
www.nickshotels-ubud.com

Pondok Taman Asri Homestay £

It is hard to believe that two people can stay overnight in such well-maintained rooms for ca. £9 a night (modern facilities with bath/WC, balcony/terrace – no air conditioning) and breakfast is also included. The location is lovely and peaceful; the town centre (where you can rent bicycles) is around 1.5km (1mi) away.
191 E4 ✉ Jl. Sri Wedari 63X
☎ 0818 05 48 74 81, no website (reservations online via sites such as www.booking.com)

Where to...
Eat and Drink

Prices
Expect to pay per person for a main course, excluding drinks and service:
£ under Rp60,000 **££** Rp60,000–120,000 **£££** over Rp120,000

There are not many restaurants that cater specifically to tourists outside of Ubud. But in Ubud itself there are hundreds of restaurants geared towards tourists, as are the majority of the places offering accommodation.

Casa Luna ££–£££

Casa Luna has been *the* meeting place for the expats living in and around Ubud for over 20 years. This means that they serve good Indonesian and Mediterranean cuisine. There is

brunch on Saturday and Sunday and music events several times a week.
191 E4 Jl. Raya Ubud
0361 97 32 82; www.casalunabali.com
Daily 9am–11pm

Clear £
Regardless of whether you are a vegetarian or vegan, enjoy macrobiotic food or prefer it raw, or are simply an omnivore – the cuisine served in the Clear offers something to suit all tastes. And, you are sure to want to come back after you have had your first meal. Especially because of the restaurant's tasteful Balinese design and décor. It is spread out over three floors and you can either sit at a table or on the floor. The service could not be more courteous and the prices – a main course costs around Rp50,000 – are astonishingly reasonable.
191 E4 Jl. Hanoman 8
0361 8 89 44 37; www.clear-cafe-ubud.com
Daily 8am–10pm

Indus ££–£££
Indus' fusion cuisine is as tasty as the service is friendly – and the view is fantastic. The dining terrace overlooks the dense tropical vegetation of the Tjampuhan River and the beautiful rice terraces. The three-course Full Moon Lover's Menu (Rp550,000 for two) is a good choice – not only on full moon nights. Friday is fish day and free tapas are served with Indus Twilight Cocktails every day from 5pm–7pm. Insider Tip
191 E4 Jl. Raya, Sanggingan
0361 97 76 84; www.casalunabali.com
Daily from 5pm

Laka Leke £–££
This restaurant has a very beautiful garden, a romantic ambience and serves delicious Balinese specialities. There are excellent dinnertime dance performances (8pm–8:45pm; on Mondays the Kecak and fire dances performances are outstanding). They also offer afternoon cooking classes. Meals cost around Rp50,000 and the menu has lots of vegetarian dishes.
191 E4 Nyuh Kuning
0361 97 75 65; www.lakaleke.com
Daily from 9am

Murni's Warung ££
This *warung* opened in 1974 and has remained a classic in Ubud ever since then. This is due to the delicious Indonesian and European cuisine, the reasonable prices and – above all – the fabulous view of the jungle valley from its four terraces. The daily specials are recommended; they include a salad (ca. Rp50,000) and main course (ca. Rp90,000).
191 E4 Jl. Raya Campuan
0361 97 52 33; www.murnis.com
Daily 9am–11pm

Where to... Shop

The entire range of Balinese arts and crafts are available in Ubud. And, if you have no inhibitions and are prepared to haggle, you will be able to buy these items at prices that would be impossible in the artisan villages. For an overview of what is on offer, take a stroll along Monkey Forest Road, Jl. Hanoman and Jl. Raya Ubud. This passes the Ubud Art Market – you will not find more Balinese souvenirs anywhere else!

Ikat Batik
This gallery supports and promotes weavers and textile artists from Bali, , making it the place to shop for top quality batiks and ikat textiles.

191 E4 Jl. Monkey Forest
0361 97 56 22; www.ikatbatik.com
Daily 10am–8pm

Jean-François Fichot
The jewellery and ornately decorated home accessories here are pure extravagance – and so are the prices.
191 E4
Jl. Raya Pengosekan 7
0361 97 46 52; www.jf-f.com
Daily 10am–5pm

Namaste
This small, but extremely well stocked, shop is the best place for those interested in spiritual matters – crystals and meditation cushions, dream catchers and incense, magnetic bracelets, essential oils, tarot cards and self-discovery books. The website provides extensive information about retreats, healing, coaching and so forth.
191 E4 Jl. Hanoman
0361 97 05 28; www.spirituality-bali.com
Daily 9am–7pm

Rio Helmi Gallery & Café
The Indonesian photographer Rio Helmi has held solo exhibitions in America and Europe and his work documents Bali (not only) from very a different perspective. There are numerous, signed photographs available to purchase.
191 E4 Suweta 6b
0361 97 23 04; www.riohelmi.com
Daily 10am–6pm

Shalimar
Masks, textiles and primitive art, shadow-puppets and sculptures, jewellery and ritual knives – this is Ubud's oldest and most trustworthy antique dealer and the best place to buy antiques from Bali and Indonesia.
191 E4 Jl. Hanoman
0361 97 71 15; www.shalimarbali.com
Daily 10am–10pm

Threads of Life
This fair trade shop has the finest collection of hand-woven textiles in Indonesia. The prices are appropriate considering that each piece is the result of months – and sometimes years – of handwork. Only natural organic dyes are used to colour the fabrics. There are textiles and woven items from Bali, Sumatra, Sumba, Flores and Timor.
191 E4 Jl. Kajeng 24 0361 97 21 87; www.threadsoflife.com Daily 10am–7pm

Where to... Go Out

FOR BODY & SOUL

Although wellness and spa services are extremely popular all over Bali, Ubud tops everything else in this regard. There are also an ever-increasing number of yoga, meditation and healing centres for visitors interested in the spiritual aspects of wellbeing. The most important event on this subject is the Balispirit Festival (www.balispiritfestival.com) that is held at the end of March/ early April every year. The recommendations are all based in Ubud.

Bali Botanica Day Spa
Spa and wellness centre a little way out of town (inexpensive transfers; free if you have least two treatments). Dozens of massages and treatments are available and various full day pamper packages are available from Rp1.2 million.
191 E4 Jl. Raya Sanggingan
0361 97 67 39; www.balibotanica.com

Bali Healers
The Balinese healing arts are rooted in age-old traditions and treats both mental and physical problems.

Several thousand traditional healers – *balians* – still practice in Bali today. It is not easy to find them yourself but your hosts/hotel will be able to help you. Most do not speak English and it is necessary to adhere to certain etiquettes. Bali Healers (http://balihealers.com) arranges sessions with healers and provides interpreters for the meetings. The service costs US$35 per hour and excludes the traditional healer's fee. Contact email: danu@earthlink.net

Taksu Healing Haven

This facility is dedicated to healing, and everything that goes along with it.
191 E4 Jl. Goutama
0361 97 14 90; www.taksuhealinghaven.com

Ubud Bodyworks Centre

Massages and holistic therapies; retreat centre and ashram are located outside of town.
191 E4 Jl. Hanoman 25
0361 97 57 20;
www.ubudbodyworkscentre.com

The Yoga Barn

Largest centre for yoga, meditation and T'ai Chi on Bali.
191 E4 Jl. Raya Pengosekan
0361 97 09 92; www.theyogabarn.com

EVENING ENTERTAINMENT

You will search in vain for thumping disco beats and an exuberant nightlife in Ubud. Evening entertainment here is more a matter of chilled live music before the lights go out at around 11pm.

Bar La Luna

This bohemian-cultural café is a meeting place for Ubud's expat community who come here to enjoy the excellent coffee, cocktails and tapas, or just to gossip, listen to the music (live music from 7:30pm several times a week) or the poetry readings. Very social. Insider Tip
191 E4 Jl. Raya Ubud
0361 97 16 05; www.casalunabali.com
Daily 3pm–11pm

Laughing Buddha

Combination of restaurant, tapas bar, cocktail lounge and music pub where there is always a great atmosphere, even after everyone else has closed up shop. There is live music every night (jazz, blues, rock and Latin) but the prices are steep, a beer costs Rp60,000.
191 E4 Monkey Forest Road
0361 97 09 28; www.laughingbuddhabali.com
Daily 9am–until late

XL Shisha Lounge

Chill out on the chairs and sofas, sip cool cocktails and smoke a shisha, chat and listen to (live music) – you can enjoy it all here.
191 E4
Monkey Forest Road 129
0361 97 57 51 Daily 11am–3am

DANCE DRAMAS

Ubud is the centre of traditional Balinese dance dramas (➤ 75), there is a performance here (or near here) every evening. They usually start at 7–8pm, the performance lasts one or two hours and costs Rp80,000–100,000. Ubud's tourist information office (➤ 78) has a calendar of events; you can also buy your tickets at the office and use the minibuses that take guests to the outlying venues.

Puri Saren

The performances on the torch-lit temple stage in the royal palace in Ubud are first-rate. They begin at 7:30pm but you should try to arrive at around 6:30pm if you want to get a front row seat; different dances are performed every day (Mon: Legong, Tue: Ramayana, Wed: Barong) and tickets are sold at the entrance.
191 E4 Jl. Raya Ubud
Daily 7:30pm–9pm Rp80,000

WORKSHOPS

Agung Rai Museum of Art
ARMA (➤ 98) is the best venue for culture workshops in Bali – be it dance or gamelan, painting or yoga, sculpture, basket weaving, batiks, woodcarving or anything else – offering almost two-dozen different workshops. Each course takes two to three hours and cost ca. US$35–50.

191 E4 Jl. Raya Pengosekan Ubud
0361 97 66 59; www.armabali.com
Daily 9am–6pm

Casa Luna Cooking School
The owner, Janet DeNeefe, is a master of Balinese-Indonesian cuisine. Her cooking courses focus on several different dishes, take three to six hours and cost Rp350,000–550,000.

191 E4 Jl. Raya Ubud
0361 97 32 82; www.casalunabali.com
Daily from 8am

Nirvana
The batik courses available in the Nirvana Guesthouse have an excellent reputation. They are held from Monday to Saturday from 9am–2/3pm. The cost for one day is Rp450,000.

191 E4 Jl. Goutama 10
0361 97 54 15; www.nirvanaku.com

Puri Lukisan
The Puri Lukisan is not only a museum housing the most important collection of Balinese art, but it also hosts workshops. There are a dozen or more courses on offer (1–5 hours for Rp150,000–500,000).

191 E4 Jl. Raya Ubud
0361 97 11 59; www.museumpurilukisan.com
9am–6pm

GUIDED TOURS & ACTIVITIES

Bali Bird Walk
There are more than 100 different bird species in the area around Ubud, including several endemic species (found only on Bali). Join one of the guided three-and-a-half-hour walks (Tue, Fri, Sat and Sun; meet at 9am at Murni's Warung, ➤ 95) to stand a good chance of seeing some of them. The walks cost US$37 including lunch.

191 E4 Jl. Raya Campuan
0361 97 50 09; www.balibirdwalk.com

Bali Nature Herbal Walk
Every day at the Museum Puri Lukisan a guided group sets off at 8:30am to explore the flora of the rural countryside. The guide points out wild herbs, medicinal plants and wild vegetables and explains how to distinguish the different plants and their various uses. Cost: US$17.

191 E4
0812 3 81 60 24 and 0812 3 81 60 20; www.baliherbalwalk.com

Banyan Tree Tours
No matter whether you want to hike through rice fields (4 hours, Rp450,000), take a leisurely cycle through Ubud's hinterland (5 hours, Rp550,000), get an adrenalin rush on a mountain bike (4 hours, Rp750,000) or go on a rafting trip (4 hours, Rp650,000) there are many operators like Banyan Tree Tours, with a great variety of activities on offer.

191 E4 Jl. Jambangan 0361 97 10 88; www.banyantreebiketours.com

Ubud Sightseeing
Every travel agency in the city has an Ubud sightseeing tour package. As a rule, the itinerary of cultural attractions takes about eight hours. The quality of these tours varies greatly. The Ubud Magic Temptation tour offered by **Perama** (Rp350,000) is good value for money and the company is a good recommendation for people interested in exploring central Bali as part of an organised excursion.

Insider Tip

191 E4 Jl. Raya Pengosekan
0361 97 33 16 and 0361 9 27 93 63; www.peramatour.com

The East

Rough Seas

The south coast of **Nusa Penida** (➤ 117) is all the more impressive for the steep cliffs that soar up 200m (650ft) but the sea is far too dangerous for swimming.

Art Village

You will be able to get an insight into classical Wayang painting, which is now rarely practiced, in the village of Kamasan, 2km (1.2mi) north of **Klungkung** (➤ 117).

Cultural Village

Experience traditional gamelan music and the Rejang dance in **Tenganan** (➤ 113), where you will feel as though you have been transported back in time.

Getting Your Bearings

The sun dances over the volcano, the scent of frangipani wafts out of the gardens and flooded rice terraces nestle picturesquely into the forested mountain slopes, which are reflected in glittering pools of water. East Bali is absolutely unique – a balm for the soul – and there is nowhere else on Bali where you can experience such tranquillity. It is the best place to recharge your batteries.

Everywhere along the coast there are long volcanic beaches and hidden coves where peaceful resorts and magnificent diving spots invite you to linger. Further inland, the rice terraces rise up to the cool heights. Picturesque villages are tucked into the steep mountain slopes and, looking through the dense green of the tropical forests, you will catch glances down to the coast where the white-crested waves break on the coral reefs. And, the gigantic cone of Gunung Rinjani seems to float above in the deep blue waters of the Lombok Straight. At 3,726m (12,224ft) this is the second highest volcano in the Indonesian archipelago and dominates Lombok just as the 3,142m (10,308ft) high Gunung Agung does the entire east of Bali. The striking rounded pyramid of this sacred stratovolcano can be seen from almost everywhere. Perched on its southwestern slope is the Pura Besakih, the mother of temples, and centre of religious life in Bali.

The omnipresent Gunung Agung (meaning "great mountain") dominates eastern Bali

TOP 10

4 Pura Besakih ➤ 104

5 Tirtagangga ➤ 109

Don't Miss

25 Padang Bai ➤ 111

26 Tenganan ➤ 113

27 Amed ➤ 115

At Your Leisure

28 Klungkung (Semarapura) ➤ 117

29 Nusa Penida ➤ 117

30 Nusa Lembongan ➤ 118

31 Candi Dasa ➤ 119

32 Amlapura ➤ 119

33 Tulamben ➤ 120

The East

Five Perfect Days

Beautiful beaches, breathtaking surf spots, snorkelling and diving, cultural attractions, holiday resorts full of contrasts and picturesque landscapes – the east of Bali is as diverse as this five-day itinerary. A rental car (with or without a driver) is the best way to explore from Padang Bai. If you are short on time you can either skip the island excursions described here – or at least those after Nusa Penida – and travel straight to Padang Bai via Klungkung.

Day 1

Morning

Take the early fast boat connection from Sanur (➤ 61; transfer from all of the tourist centres in the south) to the island of **30 Nusa Lembongan** (➤ 118), where you arrive at the ferry station in Jungutbatu after around 40 minutes. This is the starting point for a boat trip to the nearby mangroves; the return trip takes you back to Jungutbatu in time for lunch on the beach.

Afternoon

You will easily find a rental moped or bicycle and you can then ride up hill and down dale along the island's secluded paths and over the suspension bridge to **Nusa Ceningan** (➤ 119; above) where the roads are virtually traffic-free. Back on Nusa Lembongan, the route takes you, via Dream Beach and Mushroom Beach, back to Jungutbatu, where you will have no trouble finding accommodation for the night. There are many good restaurants on (and behind) the village beach where you will be able to enjoy some excellent seafood and a spectacular sunset.

Day 2

If time is not a problem, take the ferry across to **29 Nusa Penida** (➤ 117). The first boat from Jungutbatu to the neighbouring island sets out between 7am and 8am; the crossing to Toyapkeh takes around 30 minutes. When you arrive, rent a moped and take a ride around the island.

Day 3

Morning

During the high season, (fast) boats travel from the two islands to **25 Padang Bai** (➤ 111) once or twice a day. You can spend a couple of hours enjoying the beach, or snorkelling, before heading to the promenade for lunch.

Afternoon
The excursion now heads to the holiday resort of 31 **Candi Dasa** (➤ 119) and to 26 **Tenganan** (➤ 113), a culturally fascinating village that is home to Bali's indigenous inhabitants. You should allow at least two hours for sightseeing. On the way back, you can stop at the **German Bakery** (➤ 114) before ending the day in 5 **Tirtagangga** (➤ 109) – there is no lovelier place to stay on Bali than here.

Day 4

Morning
The new day begins with a dip in the wonderfully refreshing spring waters at the Tirtagangga water palace. After that, your trip takes you via 32 **Amlapura** (➤ 119) to 27 **Amed** (➤ 115), where there are a variety of restaurants for lunch.

Afternoon
Those who like snorkelling or diving should spend the afternoon enjoying the marine sights in the waters off the coast of 33 **Tulamben** (➤ 120), before spending the night in Tirtagangga or Amed.

Day 5

Morning
The early bird catches the worm…and the breathtakingly beautiful sunrise over the rice terraces en route to 4 **Pura Besakih** (➤ 104). In the morning, you also have the best chance of seeing the temple and Gunung Agung volcano before it is shrouded in clouds and mist. Start your sightseeing at around 8am and it is likely extend to around midday.

Afternoon
After lunch in the Mahagiri Panoramic Restaurant near Rendang, return to Amed. This is a good starting point for your trip to the north of Bali on the next day. However, if you decide to do a summit tour of **Gunung Agung** (➤ 166), you should spend the night in nearby Selat.

4 Pura Besakih

The Pura Besakih temple complex is perched nearly 1,000m (3,280ft) up on the southwest slope of Gunung Agung. The complex is made up of around 30 individual temples and is often shrouded in mist and clouds. It is the centre of religious life on Bali.

Built out of dark lava stone, the origins of this terrace sanctuary are lost in the mists of the pre-Hindu era. Today, it is assumed that in ancient times, this was a place where homage was paid to the god of the volcano. According to legend, the first Hindu shrine was built here on its foundation in the 8th century. It was expanded in the 13th century and from the end of the 15th century it served as the **national shrine and burial temple** for the deified kings of the Gelgel and Klungkung (➤ 117) dynasties. Since those days, each of the old royal dynasties has had its own area here, each village community and clan its own temple or shrine. There are an according number of festivities held here during the Bali year (only 210 days) – more than 70. Insider Tip If you are lucky enough to visit this mother temple during one of these festivals, you will have an unforgettable experience.

Miraculous Temple

However, most of us will never be able to experience Bali's largest and most important festival, **Eka Dasa Rudra**. This festival takes place over the course of two months when ceremonies are performed to ritually purify the entire universe. The festival is only celebrated once every 100 years and the next one is in 2063. And, hopefully there will be no volcanic activity during the festival, on the tenth day of the last centennial celebration – in March 1963 – Gunung Agung, which was thought to be extinct, erupted with great force. The disaster claimed more than 2,500 lives, destroyed dozens of villages and left more than 300,000 people homeless. But, miraculously Pura Besakih and countless worshippers were spared – the deadly lava flow changed course shortly before it reached the top temple wall.

Unforgettable Images

Traces of the lava flow that moved past the temple complex can still be clearly seen today.  Insider Tip You should not be satisfied with "only" a look at the sanctuary but rather set aside at least two to three hours

CHEATS, TOUTS, CON ARTISTS

There are two sides to every coin and the situation at the Pura Besakih temple is the flip side. There are hundreds of self-proclaimed "guides" that pounce on those tourists that arrive at the car park without a guide. They offer their services at exorbitant fees. There is no escaping them here (and in the shopping avenue leading to the temple) and when you finally reach the ticket booth – already at your wits' end – the certified employees there will also tell you a pack of lies, such as brazenly saying that the temple district can only be entered with a guide (which is true) but the prices that they quote – 500,000 or even Rp1 million – are not true yet that is what gullible tourists often pay. It is also not at all unusual to trick tourists into making payments of Rp100,000 or more by falsifying the numbers in the donation book. These tactics are all a blatant con – the only amount that has to be paid is the Rp35,000 admission fee.

Clouds and mist often envelope the 200 buildings that make up the temple complex

to spend here. That way you can explore the entire complex and experience and discover everything it has to offer. The starting point is the car park where an almost 1km (0.6mi) long avenue, lined with souvenir shops, leads straight up to the temples. It goes straight to **Pura Penataran Agung**, the spiritual centre of the entire complex. An enormous **split gate** marks the entrance, and even though tourists are not permitted to enter the main sanctuary, you should climb the staircase to the gate so that you can admire the splendid views into the temple, as well as over

The Mother Temple

The Balinese revere Gunung Agung as sacred and believe it to be the seat of the gods and the centre of the universe. It is therefore hardly surprising that the "mother" temple, Pura Besakih, was built here. The spiritual centre of the complex, the Pura Penataran Agung in which Sangyang Widi Wasa is worshipped as the incarnation of Shiva, is the template for all the 30 other temples that make up the Pura Besakih.

❶ **Split gate:** The entrance to the first of the five temple levels is at the top of a sweeping outside stairway marked by a split gate, the *candi bentar*. Lava-stone walls in varying heights separate the areas from each other. To the left and right of the gate is a bell tower (*kulkul*) where you can get a view into the inner courtyard, which is off-limits for non-Hindus.

❷ **Main courtyard:** An enclosed gate opens into the second temple level with the seat of honour and some *bale* (pavilions) where the village elders meet, where gamelan orchestras play or where offerings are prepared during festive occasions. There are two *meru* towers, one with 11 tiers and another with 9 tiers, which soar up into the sky.

❸ **Seat of honour:** The most important shrine in the entire Besakih temple complex is Sanggar Agung, a triple lotus stone throne. During the Bhatara Turun Kabeh, the colourful annual festival, this is the seat of honour for Sangyang Widi Wasa in his manifestation as the Hindu trinity of Brahma – Vishnu – Shiva.

❹ **Inner courtyards:** On the higher terraces there are a number of *bale* reserved for priestly rituals and several three- to eleven-tiered *merus* – shrines to the gods, ancestors and spirits.

❺ **Temple treasure:** The three-tiered *kehen* is used to store the temple treasures, including old wooden inscriptions.

Pura Besakih

There is a spectacular panoramic view of the surrounding countryside from the split gate

the heartland of Bali and down to the sea. This is just the first highlight; there will be many more as you make your way around the temple complex. Especially from the front side at the top, you will have a view over the entire temple complex and half of Bali stretched out at your feet.

Elaborate stone figures flank the temple area

TAKING A BREAK

There is no shortage of restaurants around the car park but it is noisy and the prices are ridiculously inflated. It is a better to idea wait a while until you get to Rendang, which is around 10km (6mi) to the south on your way back from the temple. This is where you'll find the **Mahagiri Panoramic Restaurant** (tel: 0812 3 81 47 75; www.mahagiri.com; daily from 8am), which is famed throughout the island. You can enjoy your meal with a view of the Agung on one side and the rice terraces on the other. This is a real highlight and well worth the Rp110,000 you will have to pay for the generous Indonesian lunch buffet (you can also stay overnight here but the rooms are a bit rundown and not always clean).

188 C2
Daily 8am–6pm
Rp35,000 (plus voluntary donation)

INSIDER INFO

- Morning is the best time of day to see the temple and volcano – otherwise it will be **shrouded in cloud and mist** – so you really should visit at around 8am.
- The gloriously colourful **Batara Kurun Kabeh** festival is held at the Pura Besakih temple every year in March/April. During this period, all of Bali's gods descend down from Gunung Agung to accept the offerings presented by the thousands of worshippers during the festive month.

5 Tirtagangga

Reality can sometimes be more beautiful than the picture-postcard image and such is the case at the Tirtagangga water palace. Located around 6km (3.5mi) northwest of the city of Amlapura, this is a masterpiece of horticultural design with views over the rice terraces 400m (1,300ft) below, the glittering sea and further out to the neighbouring island of Lombok.

The ponds at Tirtagangga are decorated with figures and mythological creatures

The last Raja of Amlapura was also rather fond of this vista and – as an expression of princely grandeur – he created the Tirtagangga water palace (the name means "water from the Ganges"). But, the distant holy river could not prevent the palace being reduced to ruins during Gunung Agung's last eruption in 1963. Thanks to extensive restoration work, which placed great importance on remaining true to the original, the refuge once again shines in all its former glory. The only shadow that falls on this splendid attraction is the one cast by the hordes of tourists who come here as part of their island tour from about 11am–2pm.

But even then, it is an incomparably majestic feeling to swim a few laps in the **bathing pools** of the Raja's former summer residence. The water is refreshingly cool and is said to have rejuvenating and healing powers. Glide past stone gargoyles, figures and mythical creatures that are in the shade of a magnificent banyan tree. Compared with the "water palace experience" at the weekend, when young and old frolic and create an exuberant atmosphere, even the most exquisite pool landscapes in the five-star hotels on Bali can seem rather ordinary. Insider Tip

Possibly the most unusual swimming pool in the world where refreshing water gushes out from fantastic gargoyles

Explore

Those who prefer to avoid the midday rush hour can swim in the morning or afternoon and use the rest of the time to explore the surrounding countryside. The landscape is both scenic and culturally fascinating. There are numerous hikes and walks along the small paths, trails and roads (very little traffic) that meander between the rice fields and zigzag up to picturesque lookout points, forgotten temples and idyllic villages.

The area is also ideal for more lengthy tours, especially to Tenganan (➤ 113), which makes for a wonderfully varied day. You can also set out to climb Gunung Agung (➤ 166) from here. But don't try to do it alone, as it is not easy to find the route – and most of the other paths – without the help of a local guide who knows the way.

TAKING A BREAK

There are many *warungs* at the car park in front of Taman Tirtagangga, but if you are looking for somewhere that is a bit more elegant then we have two recommendations. The first is **Tirta Ayu** (➤ 124) above the water palace, and the second is **Puri Sawah** (➤ 124), in a romantic location between the rice fields. It is renowned for its delicious Balinese dishes and its fusion cuisine.

---

189 E2 www.tirtagangga.nl
Daily 7am–6pm Rp20,000, to swim Rp10,000

INSIDER INFO

Many people consider Tirtagangga the most **beautiful retreat** on the island. Nowhere else on Bali will you find more beautiful views, or as many panoramas as here, where the hustle and bustle of south Bali and the cultural spectacle of central Bali seem to be light years away. This is the perfect place to experience the authentic, unadulterated Bali but without having to dispense entirely with the tourist infrastructure.

25 Padang Bai

It is no longer possible to find totally pristine beaches in or around Padang Bai but a touch of the "good old days", when Bali was firmly in the hands of backpackers, has been preserved here.

That is why this pleasant little fishing and beach town, which is also the harbour for the ferries to Nusa Penida and Nusa Lembongan, to Lombok and to the Gili Islands, has a reputation as the last backpacker paradise on the island. Although this claim may be rather exaggerated, it is quite obvious that the visitors to this rather charming village are more interested in taking it easy than one would expect from other resorts in Bali. They mingle with the locals over a glass of mango juice or a refreshing beer in the small *warungs* and cafés, spend the night in modest, comparatively inexpensive, accommodation, read one book after another, browse the shops for souvenirs and beach accessories and enjoy themselves sunbathing.

The perfect Balinese beach idyll awaits just outside of Padang Bai

Surrounding Beaches

However, they don't do all this right in the village, which is set on a small crescent shaped bay, because even though there is a sandy beach with clean water, it is not very peaceful. The majority of Padang Bai's residents make a living from fishing and hundreds of brightly painted outrigger

The fishing village is a pleasant place for an evening stroll

bob up and down in the shallow waters or lie on the beach where – day in, day out – fish is unloaded and nets repaired. There are also mussel-beds and strong tides, which is why most visitors prefer to head on foot to the other beaches nearby.

The most idyllic, and far and away the most popular beach is the **Blue Lagoon Beach** a few minutes' walk (follow the signposts) northeast of the village bay. The name says it all, the water here is turquoise and crystal clear and the white sand reflects the sunlight. If the swell is right, this is a great place to body surf and when its flat you can swim and snorkel at a coral reef off the coast.

However, you should always pay attention to the currents here, and at **White Sand Beach**, which the Balinese usually call Pantai Bias Tugal, around 1.5km (1mi) south of Padang Bai. This beach is good for bathing and body surfing but the waves are usually too high for snorkelling.

TAKING A BREAK

There are many cafés and restaurants along the **Jl. Silayukti beach promenade** and if you have a hankering for fresh fish, the best place is **Depot Segara** (► 124).

---

192 B4

INSIDER INFO

Besides Sanur, Padang Bai is the main harbour for the crossing to **Gili Trawangan** (► 173) and there are excursion operators in the village. The most reliable is **Perama Tours & Travel** (Dona Restaurant, Padang Bay; tel: 0363 4 14 19), which has been in the business for years. Your passage must be booked at least one day in advance – either online or by telephone (tel: 0361 75 08 08).

26 Tenganan

Tenganan is a very special place, a walled village that is home to a community of Bali Aga, Bali's indigenous population. The Bali Aga consider themselves the direct descendants of the god-king Indra and are known for their extremely conservative lifestyle.

The village maintains its original traditions and customs. It has about 300 inhabitants and is closed to motorized vehicles, and as recently as the 1960s it was still only accessible with special permission. Although it has since opened up to tourism and various modern comforts, a **complicated system of ancient rules** and ceremonies still govern this independent community. One such example is the rule regarding marriages; marriage is only permitted between village residents. Another is that any profits generated by the community must be distributed among all the village members and there is no privately owned land.

The Bali Aga celebrate the Mekare Kare festival in June/July, the festival includes a fertility rite in which young men beat each other with pandanus (screwpine) leaves

Unique Traditions

The village rice fields are also not tended by the villagers themselves but leased to the Balinese in the neighbouring villages so that the "beloved of the gods" can devote themselves entirely to the preservation of their old traditions and arts and crafts. The **geringsing textile**, which is produced by the double ikat method, is famous for being unique to this village. The most complicated individual pieces can require up to 10 years of work. In spite of their extremely high prices, these woven articles are very popular souvenirs and are offered in many shops in the village. It is also said that the fabrics protect against black magic but, as a layperson, one can never be 100% sure that the goods on sale have not been produced somewhere else.

The items available in the shops at the car park in particular are said to be inferior quality seconds. At least that's what the tourist guides say who attach themselves to those who come to the village. This can either be annoying or helpful if you want to learn more about the religious

and cultural traditions of Tenganan. It is therefore not a bad idea to join a **guided tour of the village** although this is not obligatory for foreign visitors – in spite of what you frequently read and what some guides claim.

TAKING A BREAK

At the car park at the entrance to the village there are a number of simple *warungs* serving food and refreshments but the **German Bakery** (Desa Nyuh Tebel; tel: 0363 4 18 83; daily from 8am), is considerably more pleasant, peaceful and not as crowded.

192 C5

The precious geringsing textiles are produced in small workshops in the village

INSIDER INFO

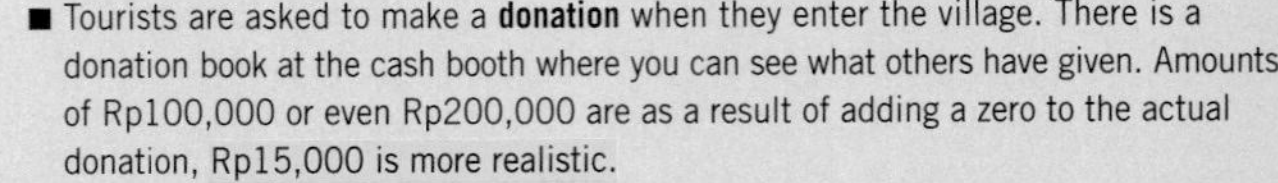

- Tourists are asked to make a **donation** when they enter the village. There is a donation book at the cash booth where you can see what others have given. Amounts of Rp100,000 or even Rp200,000 are as a result of adding a zero to the actual donation, Rp15,000 is more realistic.
- You can also visit Tenganan by **hiking** from Tirtagangga (➤ 109) and there is also a path from Candi Dasa (➤ 119) that will take you to Tenganan in about three hours. However, it is almost impossible to find these trails without the help of a local guide. Guides can be organised by accommodation places and restaurants.
- The best excursion tour company for Tenganan excursions is **JED Village Ecotourism Network** (www.jed.or.id; tel: 0361 3 66 99 51 and 0813 38 42 71 97). The company also practices sustainability and their motto is tourism "by and for the people". Guides from Tenganan lead all the tours and you can also combine a tour with a hike lasting several hours. Either way, you will get an intensive introduction into the village and its traditions "from within". The prices are rather steep – around US$75 per person (incl. transport from Ubud or South Bali).

27 Amed

There is only 14km (8.8mi) between Tirtagangga (➤ 109) and Amed – yet in such a short distance, there is a striking change in the landscape. The landscape of lush green rice terraces transforms as it gets to the coastal region, where it is semi-arid and dotted with cacti. Amed's treasures lie beneath the seawater. The coral reefs here are teeming with sea creatures, creating the perfect conditions for snorkelling and diving, where you can encounter the entire kaleidoscope of exotic marine life.

Amed is a collective name for the **small fishing villages** between Amed itself, in the north, and the village of Selang in the south. The area lies in the rain shadow of Gunung Agung, which explains the region's infertile soil. The area has always been poor and survived mainly from fishing. Tourism is therefore a very welcome source of income and slowly but surely, Amed is blossoming from an area previously only known to insiders and divers, into a new holiday centre.

However, the local beaches have grey or black sand, are sometimes pebbly and do not stretch for miles but nestle into coves. Fishing boats add a touch of colour and there are now dozens of places offering accommodation and a variety of restaurants, but the infrastructure is still underdeveloped. This is definitely not the place for you if you are looking for shops and a sizzling nightlife.

Delicate Underwater World

That said, Amed is a real paradise for snorkellers and divers, with wonderful offshore **coral gardens** of both hard and soft corals and dazzling sea creatures. Especially in the protected **Jemeluk Sea Garden**, just a stone's throw away from Amed village, snorkelling becomes an aesthetic experience whereas divers are more likely to find what they are looking for off the coast at **Lipa** and **Selang.** Only a 20-minute drive away is also **Tulamben** (➤ 120), which has become the island's second most popular dive spot – not only for exploring shipwrecks.

TAKING A BREAK

There are plenty of places to stop for refreshments but you should consider the delicious vegetarian Ayurveda meals, made with organic produce, served in the **Aiona – Garden of Health** (noon–3pm; ➤ 123), which also has a small, well-maintained **shell museum** (daily 2pm–4pm and by arrangement, admission Rp20,000).

---

189 E2

Following page: Amed's vibrant marine world

INSIDER INFO

- There are no banks in Amed or the other beach resorts but there are plenty of moneychangers that charge steep commissions. However, there are several **ATMs** in Amed.
- **Gili Sea Express** (www.gili-sea-express.com) operates a daily fast boat service from Amed to **Gili Trawangan** (➤ 173). A one-way ticket costs US$49, return is US$89 and you can book and pay online.
- **Snorkelling equipment** can be hired for about Rp45,000 a day from all accommodation places and many restaurants; **guided snorkelling and dive trips** are offered everywhere.

At Your Leisure

28 Klungkung (Semarapura)

The oldest Balinese royal dynasty was founded in **Gelgel** (just south of Klungkung) in the early 16th century by the Hindu elite who fled the neighbouring island of Java in the face of advancing Islam. The dynasty ruled well into the 18th century, and the rulers were known as Dewa Agung (meaning "sublime god"). The kingdom then collapsed and the Dutch invaded. When the Dutch attacked in 1908, the Raja saw no way out other than by committing *puputan*, ritual suicide, along with his entire royal court. The Dutch killed the survivors and also destroyed the royal palace and all the other buildings.

Today, Klungkung – which was officially renamed Semarapura in 1995 – is the capital city of Bali's eastern region. The only remains of the golden age is the **Taman Gili**, (the "garden island"), with the magnificent floating pavilion, the **Bale Kembang**, in the centre, as well as the **Kerta Gosa**, court of justice, from the 18th century. Both buildings have glorious paintings on the ceilings and roof trusses; those in the Kerta Gosa show the joys of paradise as well as drastic scenes of horror and punishment.

About 12km (7.5mi) east of Klungkung is **Goa Lawah** (daily 8am–6pm) a cave temple that is home to tens of thousands of bats.

192 A4

Klungkung Government Tourism Office
Jl. Untung Surapati 3
0366 2 14 48

Taman Gili
Jl. Puputan
Daily 9am–5pm
Rp15,000

The Kerta Gosa ceiling depicts the terrible punishments in the afterlife

29 Nusa Penida

It is only a short distance from the south coast of Bali to this island, which is about 8km (5mi) off the shore, but the change in the landscape is remarkable. While the mainland is lush and tropical, Nusa Penida has a barren karst landscape. The approximately 20km (12.5mi) long and 12km (7.5mi) wide island is actually a coral limestone plateau with spectacular cliffs, as high as 300m (1,000ft), on the southern side. The brilliant white beaches and fabulous dive spots are another highlight of the island, which only has 48,000 permanent residents. It is still relatively undiscovered and is in its infancy as a tourist destination.

Most visitors only come to the island as part of a day trip from Sanur (► 61) or Nusa Lembongan (► 118).

The mangroves at Lembongan are a verdant contrast to the beaches and dive spots

The main ferry port on the island is the fishing village of **Toyapakeh**, which has a picturesque location on a lovely sandy beach. There are also several simple places that provide accommodation, and a dive centre. It is also possible to hire motorcycles; a trip around the island will take about half a day. The road that follows the coastline in the north and east is rather desolate in some sections but passes through some impressive landscapes and several sandy beaches before making a wide arc through the hilly interior of the island, which reaches an altitude of more than 500m (1,600ft), before returning to the starting point. There are many small villages, temples and viewpoints along the way. About 6km (3.5mi) south of the main village of Sampalan, you reach the **Goa Karangsari** shrine (also: Goa Giri Putri), an approximately 400m (1,300ft) long and up to 15m (50ft) high cave that leads to an exit in a steep cliff with a view over the green valley. Near the entrance, on the right of the road, there are usually a few locals with pocket torches waiting to offer their services as guides (ca.Rp30,000).

You reach the village of **Sakti** around 10km (6mi) south of Toyapakeh and can then follow a dead-end road – sections of it are in a very poor condition – to the dazzlingly white, palm-lined **Crystal Bay Beach**. A couple of *warungs* provide refreshments and also rent snorkelling gear. There is an enchantingly beautiful coral reef just off the beach.

192 B/C1/2

30 Nusa Lembongan

Nusa Lembongan, only about 1km (0.6mi) northwest of Nusa Penida, is just 8km² (1,980 acres) in size and has around 5,000 residents in the island's three villages. The main draw cards of Nusa Lembongan include the wild surf, which attracts surfers from all around the world, its breathtaking dive and snorkelling spots, and its attractive bays. However, with only a few exceptions, most of the bays are not suitable for swimming.

Nusa Lembongan was discovered in the 1980s but until recently the island only had very spartan accommodation. Dozens of resorts, in all categories, have been developed to satisfy the increasing number of tourists, and this means that construction is still on going. However, most of the visitors come to the island on a one-day excursion from

Sanur (➤ 61). The boats usually drop anchor at the most beautiful snorkelling spots and at the beaches in the south and southwest of the island. Particularly impressive are the crescent-shaped **Mushroom Beach** (with a garden of mushroom corals off the shore), the wonderful Dream Beach (the name is really appropriate), as well as the long stretch of beach near the main tourist village **Jungutbatu**, which is popular with surfers. There are some dive centres in Jungutbatu and organised boats tours set out from the village for the **mangrove forests** that border it to the north (Rp50,000–100,000 per person).

The island is virtually car-free and if you do not want to explore it on foot, you should hire a bicycle or motorcycle (most of the tourist facilities in Jungutbatu can supply a sketch map). A narrow suspension bridge leads from Nusa Lembongan across to the little sister island of **Nusa Ceningan** (image ➤ 102) between Lembongan and Penida. This small island also attracts visitors with a few places offering accommodation and restaurants, secluded bays and the Blue Lagoon, framed by wild cliffs, at the southern tip of the island.

192 A2/3

31 Candi Dasa

"Once upon a time, there was a remote and pristine beach with sand as white as snow. It was lined with palm trees and there was a beautiful coral garden in the water, which was so crystal clear that you could make out tiny crabs in the depths..." This could be the start of a fairy tale and it was a fairy tale that came true for the first tourists who arrived here in the 1970s. But the fairy tale ended when this remote fishing village suddenly became fashionable, a second Kuta, and development and construction started. The offshore coral reef was used as construction material and as a result, the sea eroded the beach and, by the time when the madness of using coral to build with was finally stopped in 1991, the beach had almost completely disappeared. As the investors were afraid that their property could also fall victim to the tides, concrete tetrapods were used as an artificial breakwater.

The breakwater remains a handicap for the rather unspoiled holiday resort. However, with its respectable infrastructure and comparatively relaxed and peaceful holiday atmosphere, Candi Dasa is still a candidate for a stopover on a trip through east Bali, or as the starting point for exploring this part of the island.

Insider Tip

192 C4

32 Amlapura

Under the name of Karangasem, this small town became the centre of the wealthiest and most powerful kingdom on the island thanks to its

Lush lotus-blossom fields around Candi Dasa

collaboration with the Dutch. And, it must have looked magnificent until Gunung Agung erupted in 1963 and laid waste to the city. After its reconstruction, it was renamed Amlapura because the Balinese believe that a new beginning must also be symbolised with a new name.

What was designed on the drawing board is not really worth seeing but what is worth seeing is the old, renovated, royal palace, **Puri Agung Karangasem**; its mix of European, Balinese and Chinese style elements make the ensemble unique on Bali. There are several rooms and an interesting collection of old photos worth looking at.

Insider Tip It is worth making a detour from Amlapura (4km/2.5mi) to the **Puri Taman Ujung** (daily 8am–7pm) water palace, which has recently been restored.

189 E1

Karangasem Government Cultural & Tourism Office
Jl. Diponegoro 0363 2 11 96; www.tourism.karangasemkab.go.id

Puri Agung Karangasem
Jl. Sultan Agung; www.purikarangasem.com
Daily 8am–6pm Rp20,000

33 Tulamben

Its fabulous snorkelling and diving conditions more than justify making a detour to this small coastal village. It lies on a grey-black pebble beach in the middle of a steppe-like, semi-desert landscape covered mainly with succulents. Traces of the Agung eruption in 1963 can still be seen everywhere, which is why the real attractions are underwater.

Those who take the plunge will be rewarded with the captivating sight of colourful coral gardens, fascinating drop-offs, enormous schools of fish and – first and foremost – the wreck of the American merchant ship, the *Liberty*, which has been lying on the 10m–30m (33ft–100ft) deep ocean floor since the Second World War. It is only 100m (330ft) off the coast so snorkellers can also get a look at it, although exploring the interior of the wreck, now covered with corals, is exclusively the domain of divers. That is precisely what most visitors want and that is why the village's infrastructure is totally geared to divers and more than one hundred of them can be found splashing around near the wreck at any one time.

189 E3

The endangered green turtle (*Chelonia mydas*) in the waters off Tulamben

Where to... Stay?

Prices
Expect to pay per double room per night:
£ under Rp750,000 **££** Rp750,000–1.5 million **£££** over Rp1.5 million

AMED

Aiona – Garden of Health £–££

This Swiss managed eco-lodge is dedicated to sustainability, it is located right behind the beach and is set in the midst of a beautiful garden with secluded nooks. Guests feel welcome as soon as they arrive and then do not want to leave. This is partly due to the owner, Rahel, who takes great care of all her guests. And, of course, the bungalows and cottages are all individually decorated in a cosy and rustic style, as is the restaurant that is part of the complex. The entire complex is a non-smoking area.

189 F2
Bunutan
0813 38 16 17 30; www.aionabali.com

Blue Moon Villas ££–£££

There are beautiful sea views from the chic, elegant villas and penthouse rooms of this small boutique resort, as well as from its restaurant and three swimming pools.

189 F2 **Selang**
0363 2 14 28;
www.bluemoonvillas.com

CANDI DASA

Guests can choose from dozens of establishments across all categories – especially in the mid- and upper-range. The tourist traffic to Candi Dasa is still moderate, so it is often possible to snag a good deal if you are prepared to use your bargaining skills.

Anom Beach Inn £

Set in 3,000m² (32,300ft²) garden, you can choose between 8 apartments (6 price categories) and 16 surprisingly large and comfortable modern bungalows (the most romantic are in the two-storey converted rice barns). The small intimate complex borders the beach; there is a pool and a very inexpensive restaurant with a view of the sea. Tours with or without a driver are also offered (with driver £25/day).

192 C4
0363 4 19 02;
www.anom-beach.com

Bali Santi £–££

Located near the junction of the access road to Tenganan, this old hotel is right on the beach. It was recently completely renovated and some new stone bungalows (three price categories) were added. The décor is tasteful, there are modern Balinese furnishings and the rooms have large glass windows – some overlooking the sea. There are also sea views from the restaurant and swimming pool. Bookings made via an online bookings website are considerably cheaper.

Goutama
0363 4 16 11;
www.balisanti.com

NUSA LEMBONGAN

Harta Lembongan Villas £

This complex near Mushroom Bay has only been open since the summer of 2015. It offers beautiful

bungalows, built with natural materials in the traditional rice barn style, which surround the pool in a U-shape. The beach is just a few minutes' walk away.
192 A2/3
821 46 27 76 40;
www.hartalembonganvillas.com

Naturale Villas & Huts ££
This small, privately managed, eco-bungalow resort complex is set in a well-kept garden oasis. The wooden bungalows have large terraces with cosy seating areas and views of the lush greenery or the sea.
192 A2/3
0821 45 86 11 36;
www.naturalevillas.com

Tamarind Beach £–££
There are 14 stone bungalows (three price categories); the middle (deluxe) is 60m² (645ft²) and offers the best value for money. The complex's pool is directly above the beach (which is not suitable for swimming).
192 A2/3 0361 8 57 25 72;
www.balitamarind.com

PADANG BAI

Since most tourists are just passing through, and the village is geared towards backpackers, there are only two resorts but many simple bungalow complexes in the price range of £9–18.

Blue Lagoon Villa £££
Located high above Blue Lagoon Beach, this eco-boutique lodge has 25 villas with exquisite views. The panorama from the pool and restaurant is equally magnificent. Although the prices are not especially cheap by Balinese standards – a villa for up to 4 persons costs around £85 a night – they are quite justified. You will not just want to holiday like this but you will wish that you could live like this forever!
192 B4 Jl. Silayukti
0363 4 12 11; www.bluelagoon.com

TIRTAGANGGA

Cabe Bali ££
Just a 15-minute walk from the water palace, this complex has some large stone bungalows in immaculate condition. The panoramic views of the surrounding rice fields from the bungalows, pool and restaurant pavilion are absolutely breathtaking. Guests often stay longer than originally planned. There are also tour guides for hikes and walks.
189 E2
0363 2 20 45; reservations through the major bookings websites

Tirta Ayu Hotel & Restaurant £££
Built on the foundations of the former Raja palace, staying at this resort will make you feel like royalty. It is adjacent to the Tirta Gangga water palace. There is a beautiful, panoramic view over the pools and gardens from the restaurant. The five villas are luxurious and comfortably furnished in the Balinese style and with some antiques. They offer everything that a demanding traveller could desire. Massages and cooking courses are also available and – of course – there is a swimming pool.
189 E2
0363 2 25 03;
www.hoteltirtagangga.com

Villa Mega View ££
The name says it all, the view from the four residential units in the middle of the rice fields could not be better. When guests arrive they are delighted – with the view, the chic and modern apartments, the pool…simply by everything.
189 E2
81 23 91 53 32; reservations through the major bookings websites

TULAMBEN

Tauch Terminal Tulamben ££–£££
Of the many dive centres in Tulamben, the German-run Tauch Terminal is the oldest and also the one that has received the most positive client reviews. The complex is located in a well-maintained garden just behind the beach, there are two large swimming pools and the accommodation is in bungalows and rooms (all with garden or sea views). The category is upper mid-range and there is a restaurant, as well as a bar. Guests who stay and dive here can choose from several affordable packages.
189 E3 0361 77 45 04; www.tauch-terminal.com

Where to... Eat and Drink

Prices
Expect to pay per person for a main course, excluding drinks and service:
£ under Rp60,000 **££** Rp60,000–120,000 **£££** over Rp120,000

AMED

Aiona – Garden of Health £
You can pamper your body and soul by eating here, the food includes vegetarian, vegan, Ayurveda, Balinese-Indonesian, as well as Swiss-Italian. The pastas, spice mixtures, sambals and chutney are freshly made every day and the herbs and vegetables come straight out of the organic garden. And you can really taste the difference – absolutely fantastic! No alcoholic drinks are served and it is a non-smoking area.
189 F2 Bunutan
0813 38 16 17 30; www.aionabali.com
Daily from 8am, dinner reservations must be made before 3pm

Gusto Resto £–££
This restaurant is located on a hillside above the sea and has splendid, panoramic views, perfect service and an unusual Balinese-European fusion cuisine with Hungarian influences. The dishes are rather lavish and, of course, goulash is on the menu. The presentation is also a feast for the eyes. And you simply have to try the chocolate volcano for dessert – the warm chocolate cake with a liquid centre is a winner.
189 F2 Bunutan
813 38 98 13 94
Daily 3pm–10pm

Warung Celagi £
Sit in the open air, or under a palm frond roof, right on the beach and listen to the sound of the sea while you enjoy tasty Balinese dishes – especially, fish and seafood. And when it comes to paying, a main course and a drink will only cost around Rp30,000.
189 F2 Jemeluk
0859 35 02 66 19 Daily from 8am

CANDI DASA

Vincent's Restaurant ££
This looks like nothing very special from the outside but when you enter, you find yourself in a pretty

garden restaurant lit by lanterns. Romantic atmosphere, soothing jazz and fantastic French-inspired Balinese cuisine.
192 C4 Jl. Raya Candi Dasa
0363 4 13 68
Daily 11:30am–11:30pm

Warung Boni £
Charming little family-run restaurant with a handful of tables and decent Indonesian meals; most dishes only cost Rp30,000.
192 C4 Jl. Puri Bagus
818 56 52 50 Daily from 8am

NUSA LEMBONGAN

Bali Eco Deli £
It would be hard to find better smoothies in Bali than those served in this organic café! But the cakes are also almost sinfully delicious (try the apple cake with cinnamon), as are the mueslis, shakes and juices and the salads. It is a real shame that the restaurant is not open in the evening.  Definitely the place to be; especially given that the Bali Eco Deli also sees to it that hundreds of plastic bags of rubbish collected on Lembongan are removed every month.
192 A2/3 Jungutbatu, Jl. Raya
0812 37 04 92 34; www.baliecodeli.net
Daily 7am–6pm

Hai Bar & Grill ££
This beach restaurant is made entirely out of bamboo, its design and construction is so wacky that it is often more photographed than the wonderful Mushroom Bay Beach in front of it. The food is also well crafted with crisp and tasty pizzas from a wood-burning oven and super fresh seafood. Diners are prepared to pay a little more than is customary on Lembongan for such gourmet quality. And if you aren't staying in Mushroom Bay you can make use of their free shuttle service. Reservations essential.
192 A2/3 Mushroom Bay
0828 97 10 31 37
Daily 7am–10pm

PADANG BAI

Depot Segara £
Enjoy fresh fish and seafood prepared in a variety of ways as you take in the beach, promenade and harbour views from the elevated dining area.
192 B4 Jl. Silayukti 10
0363 4 14 43
Daily 8am–10pm

Ozone Café £
This restaurant is especially popular with backpackers; in the evening it is a local meeting place with music.
192 B4 Jl. Silayukti
0817 4 70 85 97
Daily 11am–1am

TIRTAGANGGA

Puri Sawah £
Right at the water palace, and in the middle of rice fields, this restaurant has beautiful views and serves some very creative, sophisticated French-Balinese cuisine. The avocado baguettes are sinfully good, as are many other dishes including the rice salad made with pieces of apple, raisins and mangos. The short walk to the restaurant starts just above the water palace car park at the right turn on the main road (signposted).
189 E2
0363 2 18 47
Daily from 8am

Tirta Ayu Restaurant ££
A majestic restaurant in a majestic hotel (► 122) – especially in the early evening when the setting sun softly illuminates the spectacular gardens and pools of the water palace.
189 E2
0363 2 25 03; www.hoteltirtagangga.com
Daily from 7am

Where to... Go Out

In eastern Bali most of the lights go out at around 10pm. Before that, visitors usually take a leisurely meal in a restaurant, listen to some music, watch a movie and sip a cocktail before letting the day come to a close on the veranda. In short: there is no nightlife to speak of in this region of Bali. Instead, you can burn off all your energy during the day, even if everything mainly revolves around diving.

AMED

Aiona – Garden of Health

Private and group meditation and yoga classes. Aiona yoga is a gentle, flowing, but still vigorous workout that is suitable for levels. A class in this lodge (➤ 121) is 80 minutes.

Amed Dive Center

This dive centre places emphasis on sustainability and has even created an artificial reef. It organises daily guided dives in Amed, Padang Bai, Tulamben and Pulau Menjangan (½ day dives Rp440,000/690,000). There are also 3-hour snorkelling tours every day (Rp225,000). Diving courses with a PADI certificate cost Rp1.12 million.

189 E2
Jl. Ketut Natih, Pantai Timur
0363 2 34 62;
www.ameddivecenter.com

Apneista

Free diving is not as easy as many people think and Amed is one of the best places to learn how to do it properly. Apneista is not only the oldest free diving school on the island but also the largest free diving centre in Southeast Asia. It offers courses at all levels, dives from the shore and from boats, as well as yoga and meditation classes.

189 F2
Jl. Ketut Natih, Jemeluk
0812 38 26 73 56;
www.apneista.com

East Bali Bike

Mountain bike tour operator with a variety of tours around Amed, they offer rides suitable for all fitness levels.

189 E2 **81 24 66 77 52;**
www.eastbalibike.com

CANDI DASA

Although the reef at Candi Dasa is no longer worth mentioning, there are many other sections of the coast with good conditions for snorkelling and diving. Most of the places that provide accommodation also rent out snorkelling gear. At the lagoon, fishermen will offer to take you out to sea in their boats to the best snorkelling spots, and there are several dive centres that compete for custom.

Bali Conservancy

This non-profit organisation is dedicated to nature conservation on Bali. Their main office is in Denpasar but they also offer several excursions from Candi Dasa including snorkelling tours, hikes and a tour to Gunung Agung's summit.

192 C4
Lobby Candi Beach Cottage & Spa
0822 37 39 84 15;
www.bali-conservancy.com

Gedong Ghandi Ashram

This ashram on the lagoon in Candi Dasa follows the principles of Gandhi and has set itself the target of guaranteeing that the region's children from less fortunate families receive a good education. That is why guests pay US$30 for their accommodation and full board (vegetarian food). You stay

in a simple bungalow and take part in the daily yoga and meditation sessions. You may also want to get involved as a volunteer. Either way, a stay in this ashram is a very relaxing and interesting experience.
192 C4 Jl. Raya Candi Dasa
0363 4 11 08, ashramgandhi@gmail.com; www.ashramgandhi.com

Sub Ocean Bali
This PADI centre also organises dive tours with no more than 4 divers at any one time (2 dives from a boat US$85, diving courses US$335).
192 C4 Jl. Raya Candi Dasa
0363 4 21 96; www.divecenter-bali.com

Trekking Candi Dasa
The English-speaking guide Somat offers an easy and informative hike through rice fields to Tenganan (ca. 1.5–2 hours, Rp225,000), as well as a more challenging tour in the mountainous hinterland of Candi Dasa (Rp350,000).
192 C4 878 61 45 20 01; www.trekkingcandidasa.com

NUSA LEMBONGAN

Nusa Lembongan is mainly visited by day-trippers from the south of Bali; Insider Tip rather than just booking the crossing, you can do an excursion around Lembongan, stop off at the most beautiful beaches, go snorkelling or visit the mangrove forests (US$50–120 per person). Snorkelling equipment can be hired at the shops on the beach at Jungutbatu for Rp30,000; several dive centres also have their offices there (snorkelling/dives Rp250,000/Rp500,000, PADI diving courses Rp3.8 million).

Big Fish Diving
This is the largest dive centre on the island and the resort also has the Yoga Shack (www.yogashacklembongan.com) that offers daily yoga classes from 8am–9:30am and 4pm–5:30pm (Rp100,000).
192 A2/3
Jungutbatu, Secret Garden Bungalows
0813 53 13 68 61; www.bigfishdiving.com

PADANG BAI

Those who want to be active in Padang Bai can go snorkelling or diving. The accommodation places usually also provide snorkelling equipment for around Rp30,000. The fishermen at the beach offer snorkelling excursions (ca. Rp100,000 for 2 persons for 2–3 hours).

Geko Dive
The oldest dive centre in Padang Bai; two dives cost Rp1.125 million.
192 B4 Jl. Silayukti
0363 4 15 16; www.gekodive.com

TIRTAGANGGA

All accommodations and restaurants also organise guides for hikes into the countryside surrounding Tirtagangga (ca. Rp80,000/hour for 1–2 persons).

Bungbung Adventure
Mountain bike tours from 2–6 hours start at Rp350,000. They set out from the entrance to the water palace. It is also possible to hire guides for a Gunung Agung (► 166) ascent (ca. Rp1.5 million for 2).
189 E2 0813 38 40 21 32

TULAMBEN

Snorkelling equipment costs ca. Rp30,000–45,000, two dives for ca. Rp850,000, an unlimited number of dives on a single day Rp1.5 million and PADI diving courses for around Rp5 million. The **Tauch Terminal** (► 123) has the best reputation; people not staying in the house can take a shower for a fee. Daily dive trips to Amed, Nusa Lembongan and Nusa Menjangan.

The North

Little Treats

Berry Nice

It's all about the locally grown juicy, sweet red berries at the Strawberry Stop on the main road in Candikuning, which is on the edge of the **Danau Bratan** (➤ 137).

The Journey is the Destination

Follow the road that runs from **Kedisan** (➤ 132) to Abang and you can then take a scenic walk along the lakeside to the village of Trunyan.

Unusual Relief

In Kubutambahan, near **Singaraja** (➤ 143), is the Pura Meduwe Karang where you'll find a bas-relief of a European man riding a bicycle.

Getting Your Bearings

It is a truly cinematic panorama – dark lava, lunar landscapes around the Batur Volcano, misty rainforests, crater lakes shimmering in intense shades of green and blue, the rainbow spray of waterfalls, the glassy Bali Sea, with its incredible coral gardens, against the backdrop of black sand – the scenery in north Bali really is Oscar worthy.

In picturesque north Bali there is something new to see at every turn and, as such, this region is known for its breathtaking nature experiences (although there are also many cultural attractions). Endless beaches stretch along the pristine coast while the interior rises up steeply to over 2,000m (6,560ft) with one of the most

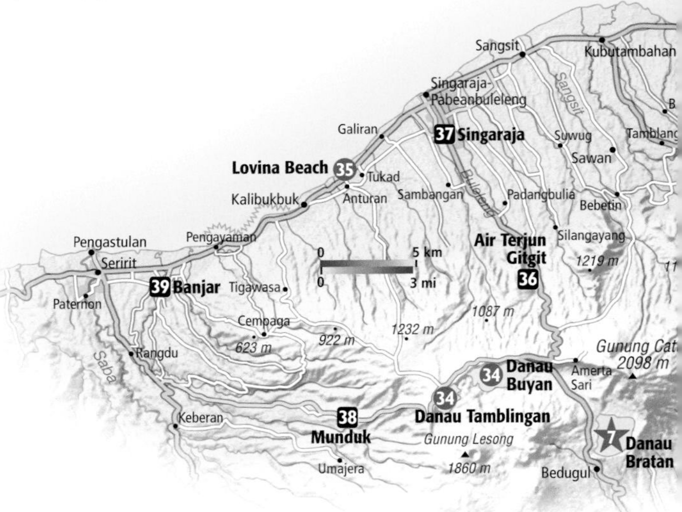

Balinese contrasts: dark sandy beaches...

...and dense, lush rain- and cloud forests shape the landscape

spectacular volcanic landscapes on our planet, alongside the lush greenery of the rain- and cloud forests. The climate becomes cooler and more pleasant with each step upwards, the morning dew lies on green meadows, mist and low-lying clouds envelope the hilly landscape where extensive fields of strawberries flourish. Time and time again panoramas, which are unrivalled on Bali, unfold before your eyes.

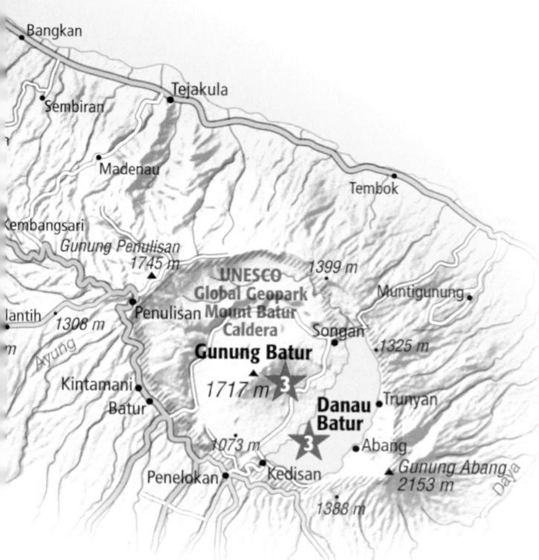

TOP 10

- 3 Gunung Batur & Danau Batur ➤ 132
- 7 Danau Bratan ➤ 137

Don't Miss

- 34 Danau Buyan & Danau Tamblingan ➤ 139
- 35 Lovina Beach ➤ 141

At Your Leisure

- 36 Air Terjun Gitgit ➤ 143
- 37 Singaraja ➤ 143
- 38 Munduk ➤ 144
- 39 Banjar ➤ 145

The North

Five Perfect Days

You should plan on spending at least four days – and an extra morning – for your tour through north Bali. This is not only due to the mountain roads – some are very narrow and progress is slow – but also to give you enough time to fully appreciate the unique volcanic landscape in this part of the island. A rental car, with or without a driver, is essential.

Day 1

Morning

Start your journey of discovery with a ride to the roof of Bali. One scenic panorama follows another on the drive between Penelokan and Penulisan, at an altitude of more than 1,400m (4,600ft), to one of the world's largest calderas. ★3 **Gunung Batur** and **Danau Batur** (► 132) make the fascinating setting perfect.

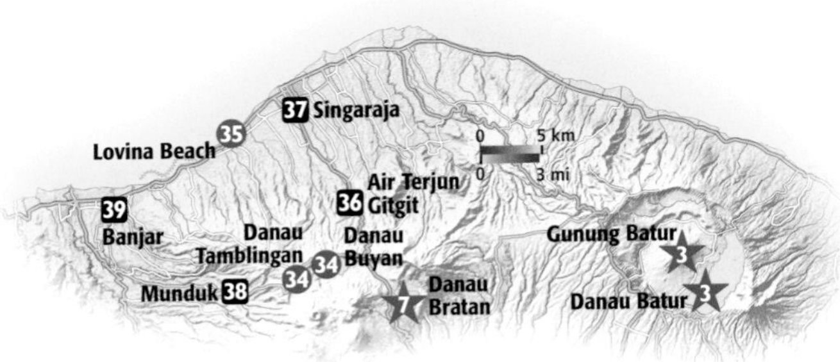

Afternoon

Sometimes less is more: follow the shore road to the end, take a tour of the lake and spend the rest of the day marvelling at the surrounding beauty.

Day 2

Morning

Today, you will have to get up early and set out at around 3am in order to reach the summit of **Gunung Batur** (► 132) before sunrise. Once you are standing on the peak watching the sun as it rises up over Lombok, you will feel justly rewarded for the effort of the ascent. After the descent and a refreshing shower, you can enjoy a second breakfast and a nap in Penelokan.

Afternoon

Your drive along the crater rim takes you to Penulisan, after which the road goes steadily downhill. With the sea always in sight, you reach

Kubutambahan and then go along the coast to **37 Singaraja** (➤ 143). On your way back to the interior of the island, you pass the **36 Air Terjun Gitgit** (➤ 143) waterfall before reaching the highest point of the tour at Wanagiri. Then it is down to today's destination, Danau Bratan.

Day 3

Morning

To see the sunrise over ★7 **Danau Bratan** (➤ 137) you have to have another early start to the day. It is a sublime sight to see the temple towers of the Pura Ulun Danu Bratan standing out against the glowing sky. No less beautiful are the **Kebun Raya Eka Karya** (➤ 138) botanical gardens to the south. Couple this with a picnic of the fresh fruit you bought in **Candikuning** (➤ 138; above) – perfect!

Afternoon

There are many attractive accommodation options and excellent restaurants near the twin lakes of **34 Danau Buyan** and **Danau Tamblingan** (➤ 139), especially in nearby **38 Munduk** (➤ 144).

Day 4

Morning

The landscape changes continuously on the 20km (12.5mi) drive from Munduk down to the coast near Seririt. You now follow the main road to the right and will soon see the signpost for **39 Banjar** (➤ 145). Your first stop there should be the Brahma Vihara Arama before continuing on to the hot springs at Komala Tirta.

Afternoon

You really deserve a lazy afternoon on the beach at **35 Lovina** (➤ 141) where you can choose between dozens of restaurants for dinner.

Day 5

No stay in Lovina would be complete without taking part in a dolphin-watching tour. It is all over by about 9am so you will have plenty of time to enjoy a good breakfast and spend the rest of day relaxing.

3 Gunung Batur & Danau Batur

With an altitude of 1,717m (5,633ft), the cone-shaped Gunung Batur may not be the highest volcano on the island, but it is the most active. It rises up in the centre of a 10km × 13.5km (6mi × 8.4mi) large outer caldera. Nestled beside it are the deep blue waters of Danau Batur, the largest lake on Bali, forming one of the world's most spectacular volcanic landscapes.

At the moment it is only simmering on a low flame but there are clear indications – the barren lava fields at its base, the numerous hot springs and hissing fumaroles on its flanks and the occasional rising wisps of smoke that rise up above its several craters – of the dormant volcanic forces that could be released at any time. There have been more than 20 eruptions in the past 200 years.

Along the Crater Rim

The streams of molten lava from the eruptions destroyed several villages in the interior of the gigantic caldera, which was created millions of years ago. After the 1963 eruption a village had to be evacuated and it was subsequently rebuilt on the rim of the crater. It was named Penelokan, which means "beautiful view", and it is indeed hard to imagine a more beautiful panorama. The village is located at an altitude of 1,452m (4,763ft) so the view takes in the caldera, the crater lake and the cone of the volcano. The numerous inns and lodgings all vie for custom by promising the best view. If you are interested in volcanism you should pay a visit to the **Museum Gunung Api Batur**.

About 6km (3.5mi) further along the crater rim road is the village of **Kintamani** and the **Pura Ulun Danu Batur** temple. The views are breathtaking but they get even better. Another 5km (3mi) further along is **Penulisan**, which marks the highest point (1,650m/5,413ft) accessible by road on Bali. If that is not enough, you can set out on foot to explore and climb up the 333 steps to the **Pura Tegeh Koripan.** It is perched high above the landscape at an altitude of 1,745m (5,725ft), making it Bali's highest temple that even overtakes the Gunung Batur by 32m (105ft) and the Danau Batur crater lake by more than 600m (2,000ft).

On the Lake Shore

Driving down to the lake is a must for all tourists even those who do not plan to climb the **Batur Volcano** (► 169). After Penelokan, the road (signposted Kedisan) zigzags its way steeply down to the shore of the lake, which is one of the largest of its kind on earth and over 100m (330ft) deep.

The peaceful idyll is deceptive: Gunung Batur's eruptions in 1917 and 1926 claimed more than 1,000 lives and are considered the worst in history

Bali's Volcanic Heart

The island of Bali (5,561km²/2,147mi²) is volcanic in origin and it is the most western island in the Lesser Sunda Island group in the Indian Ocean, between Java and Lombok. It is also on the Ring of Fire that encircles the Pacific and spans nearly 40,000km (24,855mi) (➤ 22) in length. The highest point on the island is the active volcano, Gunung Agung, which has an altitude of 3,142m (10,308ft). The volcano, which the Hindus regard as sacred, last erupted in 1963. Only a just over half as high, but no less impressive, is Gunung Batur further to the west. The volcanoes are the most defining elements of Bali's topography.

Gunung Batur & Danau Batur

❶ Central Bali: The central region of Bali is dominated by four volcanic complexes with the highest, Gunung Agung, in the eastern part of the island. The transitional zone to north Bali is marked by Gunung Batur (1,717m/5,633ft) with an impressive crater lake, which is the largest of its kind in the world. The Catur (2,096m/6,876ft) and Batukau (2,276m/7,476ft) volcanoes are further to the west.

❷ West Bali: The narrow western section of the island, with the Bali Barat National Park (➤ 158), is characterised by deep valleys and mountain ranges that were formed during the Tertiary Period. This region lies on the leeward side, protected by the mountains, and is therefore considerably drier the south of Bali.

❸ South Bali: This area of Bali is the most fertile part of the island, with moist earth deposits made fertile by volcanic ash. These lie on the windward site of the central volcanic range, which slopes down to the south and benefits from high rainfall throughout the year. This is the island's most intensively farmed agricultural region.

❹ East Bali: The mountain ranges of central Bali extend down close to the edge of the island and determine the landscape. The omnipresent Gunung Agung (➤ 106) with its foothills spreading out in a north-south direction, and Gunung Batur, whose massif forms the transitional zone to central Bali, dominate the landscape in this part of the island.

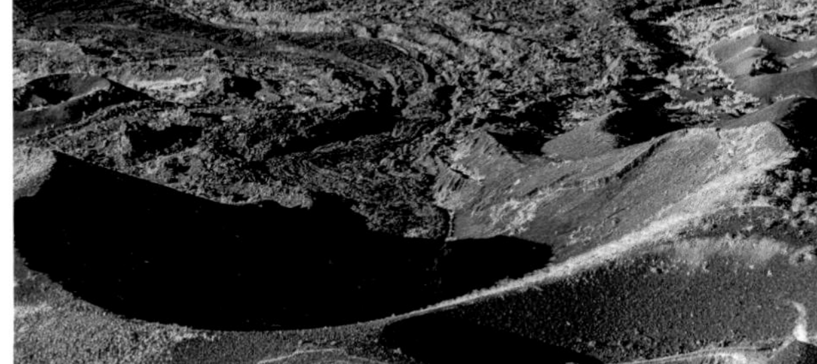

Lunar landscape on the Gunung Batur

BEWARE
Almost all of the guided tours make stops for photos, to have lunch or just to go shopping in Penelokan and/or Kintamani and the touts and souvenir sellers in the two villagers are even more annoying than in most other places. You will need a thick skin not to flee – as many other tourists do – when dozens of vendors descend on you and children surround you shouting "money, money" at the top of their voices.

From **Kedisan**, where it is also possible to spend the night, the road winds its way through bizarre fields of solidified lava to **Toya Bungkah**, the starting point for a trek to Gunung Batur, which starts out early in the morning, and for boat trips on the Danau Batur. The rather shabby spas in the village are not worth a mention and the boat trip to Trunyan, a village with Bali's indigenous people, is also not worth the rather steep price. However, a short **lake cruise** and the aforementioned ascent of the volcano are both unforgettable experiences.

TAKING A BREAK
In Penelokan and Kintamani, dozens of run-of-the-mill restaurants lie in wait for busloads of tourists. The buffet lunches they all offer range from just plain insipid to very bad, and they are overpriced. In contrast, the food served in the **Lakeview Restaurant** (► 146) in Penelokan, as well as in the **Puklu Mujung Warung**, a few metres further along the way to Kintamani, is reasonably good (both open at around 7am/8am). An even better idea is to go to the market at Kintamani and buy some fruit and enjoy a picnic with a panoramic view.

---

188 B3

UNESCO Global Geopark Mount Batur Caldera
Penelokan
Rp15,000 per person (paid at the entrance to the village; the ticket is valid for the entire vicinity so take good care of it)

Yayasan Bintang Danu
Penelokan 0366 5 17 30
Daily 10am–3:30pm (private information centre run by dedicated villagers)

Museum Gunung Api Batur
Penelokan 0366 5 11 86
Daily 9am–5pm Rp10,000

Pura Ulun Danu Batur
Kintamani
Daily 8am–6pm Rp15,000

Pura Tegeh Koripan
Penulisan
Daily 8am–6pm Rp10,000

7 Danau Bratan

No matter which direction you approach it from, you cannot help but be impressed by the landscape around Danau Bratan. The lake covers 4km² (990 acres) and is as deep as 30m (100ft). Together with the neighbouring lakes, the Buyan and Tamblingan (► 139), it lies in the midst of a huge former volcano crater at an altitude of around 1,200m (4,000ft). Its flanks rise up to a height of 2,000m (6,500ft) and are covered with a dense mountain rainforest forming impressive scenery in every shade of green imaginable.

The small lake temple on the western shore of Lake Bratan

When you see this scenic landscape, you will understand why the Balinese consider the Danau Bratan to be sacred. You should make every effort to spend at least one night here, even if it is only to see the sunrise over the lake and the **Pura Ulun Danu Bratan**, which appears to float on the water. The park surrounding the temple complex is dedicated to the lake goddess and it is a breathtaking sight to watch as the first rays of the sun touch the plants – dazzling bougainvillea, blood-red lilies and sparkling white gardenias covered in morning dew. And then along the lakeside, you can watch as the sun warms the lotuses, with their white and pale pink buds, as they start to open up, just like a slow-motion film sequence.

Insider Tip

Into the Lush Greenery

As the day progresses, the light loses its intensity and the almost mystical atmosphere of the early morning gives way to one that is far busier. This is due to the busloads of tourists that arrive to visit the lake and temple every day at 8am. Soon, noisy motorboats appear and the souvenir sellers start peddling their wares – high time to move on into the vast green expanse of the **Kebun Raya Eka Karya** botanical gardens, which is touted in the brochures as one of Bali's most beautiful natural attractions. And, if your feet need a break you can opt instead to drive through the garden.

Opened in 1959, it is the oldest botanical garden (not founded by the Dutch) in Indonesia and with an area of 160ha (395 acres) one of the largest in the country. No less than ca. 2,000 plant species grow here; they include 800 different trees and 400 varieties of orchids that are displayed in the orchid house, where 27 butterfly species flutter around them. There is also a cactus house.  Not only nature lovers will be delighted to spend time in the gardens, with its well marked trails, clear information labels, lotus pond and small temple.

Casuarina forests in the Kebun Raya Eka Karya botanical gardens

TAKING A BREAK

Near the temple is the village of Candikuning, which has a morning market that is well stocked with an astonishing variety of fruit. This is the perfect place to buy delicious fruits – strawberries, bananas, papayas, pineapples and mangos – for a lunchtime picnic in the botanical gardens.

---

187 E3

Pura Ulun Danu Bratan
Candikuning, Danau Bratan
Daily 7am–6pm Rp30,000, car park Rp5,000

Kebun Raya Eka Karya
Candikuning 0368 2 03 32 11; www.kebunrayabali.com
Daily 7am–6pm
Rp20,000; cars additional Rp15,000, car park Rp6,000

INSIDER INFO

People looking for a real thrill should head for the **Bali Treetop Adventure Park** that is integrated into the botanical gardens. The different zip lining and climbing circuits guarantee an adrenalin rush and are fun for the whole family (Kebun Raya Eka Karya; tel: 0361 9 34 00 09; www.balitreetop.com, admission US$22–28).

34 Danau Buyan & Danau Tamblingan

As with Danau Bratan (➤ 137), the lakes further to the northwest – Buyan and Tamblingan – fill the deepest depression in a gigantic caldera, and were formed by the collapse of a volcano millions of years ago.

A handful of small villages and solitary temples are the only man-made elements on the lake's shallow, pristine shores. The area is wonderful for hiking; **an easy hike** starts at the Danau Bayan car park, where a road branches off in the small market village of Pancasari north of Danau Bratan. It leads along the southern shore of Danau Buyan, and then crosses a mountain ridge before going down to the smaller Danau Tamblingan and then up to the village of Tamblingan. The route is just under 4km (2.5mi) but you should count on it taking a good two hours. And, it is a great advantage if you have a car with a driver, as they can then pick you up at the end of the hike.

Panoramic Views...

...of both lakes can also be enjoyed from your car window when you take the high road **above the lakes**, which branches off from the main road to the west at the Wanagiri Pass. Over the next few kilometres, you will be able to enjoy fantastic views of the endless expanse of the ocean to the north and, looking to the south, you will catch glimpses of the glittering turquoise and blue waters of the lakes through the dense green of the jungle.

Traditional wooden boats on the shore of Lake Tamblingan

The turquoise waters of Lake Buyan

The road eventually leads to the village of **Tamblingan** and it is then only a 10-minute walk from the car park down to the lakeshore. There are guides at the car park who offer a variety of tours. It is also possible to spend the night here in simple lodgings but there is a far broader spectrum of accommodation in Munduk (➤ 147), which is only a short drive away.

TAKING A BREAK

There are several **strawberry fields** near Danau Buyan where children and adults alike can have some fun picking their own strawberries. A bag only costs around Rp30,000, which is a real saving as you pay about twice as much for the fruit if it has already been picked. There is no lack of strawberry farms – they extend all along the road from Pancasiri to the Danau Buyan.

187 D3

INSIDER INFO

The entire region around the twin lakes is ideal for walks and **longer hikes**; it is also possible to undertake **full-day volcano climbs** from here. The main centre of hiking tourism is the village of Tamblingan. The tour guides all offer similar deals: a group of up to four people costs around Rp350,000 for 90 minutes; Rp500,000 for three to four hours and about Rp750,000 for a full-day tour.

35 Lovina Beach

It is now more than 60 years since Anak Agung Panji Tisna, the Raja of Buleleng, had the foresight to put up a couple of simple palm frond huts on his beach property, 5km (3mi) west of Singaraja, and call it Lovina.

Today, the name refers to an approximately 12km (7.5mi) stretch of coast with half a dozen holiday villages – and it is still growing. The largest and best known is **Kalibukbuk** that consists of nothing but lodgings and restaurants, shops and travel agencies – and the same applies to all the others. The main thoroughfare, which has a view of the rice fields and central mountain range, runs into the hinterland away from the ocean. The beach that stretches for miles along the coast is rather unspectacular with dark sand, pebbles and sharp coral fragments. But the sea is glassy and the offshore **coral reef** offers good conditions for snorkelling in pleasantly warm water. There is no night-life worth talking about and the atmosphere is generally relaxed and rather peaceful. The comparatively low prices draw many backpackers and individual tourists who are joined by crowds of day-trippers from the south of the island that show up here in the early morning as part of their organised tours.

Dolphin Watching

Dolphin watching is the main tourist attraction in the far north of Bali. Tours start just before sunrise when dozens

When the fishermen return in their outriggers they sell their catch to vendors on Lovina Beach

of slim, traditional outriggers – powered by loud rattling outboard motors – set out from the beach with their load of tourists and head out to sea. Their destination is the coral reef about 9km (5.5mi) off the coast where several schools of dolphins arrive shortly after dawn in search of food. The engines roar, there is the smell of petrol and exhaust fumes in the air and yet (surprisingly) the mammals don't seem undisturbed by this "dolphin hunt" that has been taking place for years. The dolphins catch fish while the tourists snap away until their memory cards are full, knowing that the whole hubbub will soon be over. After about two hours, you'll be back on dry land where you can spend the rest of the day lazing on the beach or snorkelling at the reef.

TAKING A BREAK

Done out entirely in green, the comfortable and airy **Akar Café** is the best place in north Bali for vegetarians, vegans and all those who appreciate food that has been sustainably produced. They serve the creamiest smoothies, the home-made ice cream is a treat, and the main courses and salads, coffee and desserts are also delicious.

The dolphins seem unperturbed by the tourist boats

186 C4/5

INSIDER INFO

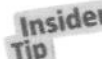

- The roads to the south and west of the Jl. Raya Lovina are ideal for cyclists. There is relatively little traffic and the scenic **bike trails** run through picturesque rice terraces, hills and mountains, with wonderful views of the surrounding countryside and the Pacific. Bicycles can be hired everywhere at prices starting at Rp20,000 per day.
- **Bali Vespa Tour** (tel: 0877 62 45 77 72; www.bali-vespa-tour.com) offers really fascinating – but unfortunately rather expensive – customised tours. You can hire a lovingly restored and maintained **vintage Vespa** (1 hour: Rp120,000, each additional hour: Rp100,000), or join a scooter tour (with accompanying vehicle) to a variety of local attractions, such as a shopping trip to Singaraja (6 hours: Rp510,000). Their range also includes a cooking course (4 hours: Rp510,000) and about a dozen treks in the area surrounding Munduk (6–9 hours: Rp510,000–850,000).

At Your Leisure

36 Air Terjun Gitgit

Air Terjun means "waterfall" and Gitgit, around 11km (7mi) south of Singaraja on the steep route to Danau Bratan, is considered to be Bali's most beautiful waterfall, and it is certainly marketed accordingly. You can't miss all the Gitgit signposts, let alone the dozens of souvenirs shops, stalls, restaurants and refreshment kiosks that line the 15-minute walk from the car park to the waterfall. The touts that loudly advertise their goods may get on your nerves, the noise abates as you approach the falls, only to be replaced by the sounds of the raging water. The torrent plunges about 35m (115ft) down into a rocky pool surrounded by jungle – a dip in the water or just a brief shower from the spray is a pleasant way to cool off. This will be so refreshing that you will find it easier to tolerate all the tourist hullabaloo and you'll be relaxed enough to admire the wonderful panoramas and the view of the distant blue ocean.

Daily **Rp10,000**

A refreshing dip in the pool at the Air Terjun Gitgit waterfall

37 Singaraja

This is the second-largest town (more than 130,000 inhabitants) in Bali, and the economic centre of the entire north of the island. The town's name, which means "lion king", harks back to a time in history when Singaraja was an important trading centre and royal seat. As far back as the 10th century, the town had commercial contact with China and India. From the 16th–19th century it was the **seat of power of the Raja of BuluIeng** before being conquered by the Dutch in 1849. From this time on, until 1946, Singaraja remained the island's capital, and seat of Dutch colonial power, which ruled the whole of the Lesser Sunda Islands area until 1953. The powerful Dutch East India Company, which controlled the spice route, also had its headquarters here. Broad avenues, colonial buildings and large warehouses are just some of the remnants of this era; there are many other traces, especially in the vicinity of the **old port**.

The port area is dominated by the impressive **Independence**

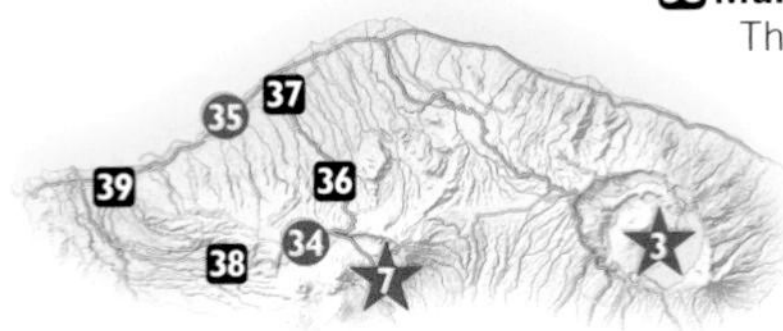

Monument and, opposite it, the exotic colours of the Chinese Temple. The other attractions in Singaraja are a little inland, close to the main thoroughfare. In the historic library, the **Gedung Kirtya,** there are no less than 4,000 *lontars*, traditional "books" made of dried palm leaves. They embody Bali's literary heritage and the country's the oldest written records are also preserved in the library. In addition, there are thousands of books, magazines and newspapers from the period of the Dutch occupation.

187 D5

Buleleng Government Tourism Office
Jl. Veteran 23 0362 6 11 41
Mon–Fri 8am–3:30pm

Gedung Kirtya
Jl. Veteran 20 Mon–Thu 8am–4pm, Fri until noon Free (donation requested)

38 Munduk

The location of this small village is absolutely stunning. At an altitude of 700m (2,300ft) it is nestled in the lush greenery of the northern slopes of the central mountain range. Its location alone was reason enough for the Dutch to build their retreats here so they could escape the sweltering heat of the lowlands. Today, wealthy Balinese – and tourists – appreciate not only the pleasant climate but also the breathtaking panoramic views through the greenery down to the glittering sea. The **countless hiking trails** around Munduk lead through "tamed" jungle to coffee and cocoa, fruit and clove plantations and further afield to Danau Buyan and Danau Tamblingan (► 139) as well as dozens of waterfalls. All of the places offering accommodation will offer advice and directions (usually hand-drawn maps) and there are guides waiting to show tourists all the highlights that nature has in store.

186 C3

There are excellent hiking trails and footpaths in the area surrounding Munduk

The only Buddhist monastery in Bali is near the small village of Banjar

39 Banjar

This villiage is ideal if you need a change from all of the rather inconspicuous exteriors of the Balinese Hindu temples. Here you will find a magnificent building with ornate halls and dazzling golden pagodas, with colourful statues under impressive arches. Here in Banjar, not far from the beach but in an idyllic location on the edge of rice terraces, you will discover the only Buddhist monastery on Bali, the **Brahma Vihara Arama** complex. It was built in 1972 with funding from Thailand and its many playful details show that it was modelled on similar Thai complexes. A guide – a monk in a yellow robe – takes great pleasure in accompanying visitors from the splendid lotus pond through the individual rooms (take your shoes off before you enter!), to *stupas* and shrines, meditation pavilions and the monks' cells, and the monastery garden with a model of the **Borobodur Temple** on the neighbouring island of Java. There is an atmosphere of silence and meditative calm, and those who are interested (and have enough time) can take classes in the art of Vipassana meditation during a 10-day retreat.

On the return journey to the coast, you will see signposts for the **Air Panas Komala Tirta** (also: Air Panas Banjar), hot springs. Set in the midst of tropical vegetation, this is another place of tranquillity and reflection. The natural hot springs form three pools with the water bubbling down from one basin into the next where you can float in the steamy 38 °C (100°F) water, which is rich in sulphur and potassium, and listen to the sounds of the jungle. The warm waters are believed to have great healing powers and bring relief to skin conditions and arthritis. A small restaurant is attached to the complex and lockers are also available.

186 B4

Brahma Vihara Arama
Banjar Tegeha;
www.brahmaviharaarama.com
Daily 8am–6pm donation requested

Air Panas Komala Tirta
Banjar Tegeha
Daily 8am–6pm
Rp10,000

Where to... Stay?

Prices
Expect to pay per double room per night:
£ under Rp750,000 **££** Rp750,000–1.5 million **£££** over Rp1.5 million

DANAU BATUR

Baruna Cottages £
These rice barn style bungalows are in a beautiful location on the lakeshore; the complex would have even more to offer if it was properly maintained. It is fine to spend the night given that volcano climbs are also available.
188 B3 **Buahan (near Trunyan)**
0366 5 13 78; www.barunacottages.com

Batur Mountain View £–££
Situated 2km (1.2mi) before Kintamani, on a steep slope above Danau Batur, this hotel's big draw card is the views of the volcano and lake. The rooms are rather sparsely furnished but some do have the all-important view. Organised volcano tours.
188 B3 **Jl. Culali** **0877 62 59 65 03; www.baturmountainview.com**

Lakeview Eco Lodge £–££
Back home a night in a hotel in a location such as this one would cost a fortune but here you can stay in a backpacker dormitory for ca. £17, or in one of the rooms with balcony – there are three categories – starting at £35. Naturally, the complex also has a restaurant with panoramic views.
188 B3 **Penelokan**
0366 5 25 25; www.lakeviewbali.com

Surya Hotel £
Surya is just across the street from Danau Batur. It has very basic rooms and bungalows that are not always clean. Everything is a bit rundown; treks up Batur are also offered here.
188 B3 **Jl. Kedisan, Lake Batur**
0366 5 13 78; www.suryahotel.com

DANAU BRATAN

Bali Handara Kosaido Country Club £££
This hotel boats views of the "most beautiful golf course on earth" and some people are also prepared to pay up to US$300 (the most expensive chalet) to see those views. The standard rooms, which are decorated in warm tones, are worth the US$100 rate.
187 E3 **Bali Handara Golfclub, Pancasari**
0362 3 42 26 46; www.handaragolfresort.com

Enjung Beji Resort Villa £–££
Mid-range establishment with stone bungalows (three price categories) close to the Pura Ulun Danu Bratan.
187 E3 **Jl. Raya Bedugul**
0852 85 21; www.enjungbejiresort.com

Puri Candicuning Retreat £££
This top class villa complex is near to Pura Ulun Danu Bratan and is situated right on the lake. Even the smallest and least expensive villa (ca. £80 via a booking website) has more than 80m² (860ft²) of living space with a kitchen, living, dining and bedroom, bathroom with Jacuzzi and a huge veranda. The villas are all decorated with exquisite artefacts, there is also a jogging course, a library and billiard room; the restaurant serves Balinese and international cuisine.

187 E3 Jl. Raya Candficuning
0368 2 03 32 52; www.puricandicuning.com.

Strawberry Hill Hotel ££
Set in gardens, with views of the strawberry fields, these 17 rustic bungalows are made of natural materials. Some have an open fireplace and are exceptionally comfortable but still modern. Highly recommended!
187 E3
Jl. Raya Denpasar-Singaraja, at km 48
0368 2 12 65; www.strawberryhillbali.com

MUNDUK

There is plenty of accommodation in all categories on offer in this up-and-coming holiday village. They all have one thing in common – they offer much better value for money than comparable places at nearby Lake Bratan.

Aditya Homestay £
The modern house is rather non-descript from the outside but has pleasant, functional rooms. The rooms all have large glass fronts onto a balcony, and spectacular views. The owner is also very amiable (he provides maps to help guests find the waterfalls and other services), the breakfast is plentiful and varied and the meals served in the restaurant are above the average. In this instance, it is actually cheaper to make your reservation via their own website. Rooms cost US$25–29, depending on the season.
186 C3 Jl. Pura Buseh
0852 38 88 29 68; www.adityahomestay.com

Lesong Hotel ££
Set back from the main road, this new building nestles picturesquely on a lush green slope. The elegant rooms are decorated with high-quality wooden furniture, have large glass windows and generous balconies with panoramic views. The Balinese food served in the restaurant is fantastic. If you need a guide for your hikes, just ask Nyoman, the endearing manager of this highly recommended hotel, where you are sure to feel at home.
186 C3 Banjar Gesing
0859 65 94 45 22; www.lesonghotel.com

Puri Lumbung Cottages ££–£££
The 35 bungalows of this sustainably managed complex are either painstakingly restored *lumbung*, traditional Balinese rice barns, or exact replicas. It is hard to imagine a more authentic and romantic place to stay in Munduk. Activities – such as cooking and dance classes, carving, flute and yoga courses, hikes and bicycle tours – will guarantee that you are never bored even if you decide on a longer stay.
186 C3 Banjar Taman
81 23 87 40 42; www.purilumbung.com

LOVINA

Adirama Beach Hotel & Restaurant ££
This complex, which is located a little to the west of Kalibukbuk centre, between the road and sea, is under Dutch management. The 25 rooms have views of the garden, pool or sea. Some of them are a little worse for wear, so you should inspect them before you sign in.
186 C5 Jl. Raya Singaraja-Seririt
0362 4 17 59; www.adiramabeachhotel.com

Banyualit Spa 'n Resort £–££
Charming, family-run beach hotel in a landscaped tropical garden with a surprisingly large swimming pool. The cottage style rooms come with air conditioning (or a fan) but the villas – especially the Deluxe category (Rp800,000) – offer the best value for money. The restaurant serves excellent food and there are reasonably priced treatments available in the attractive spa.
186 C5
0362 4 17 89; www.banyualit.com

Rambutan Boutique Hotel £–££

Situated a five-minute walk away from the beach, this complex is set in 2ha (5 acres) of lush gardens with two pools. The rooms (five price categories) all have either a terrace or balcony, and all offer exceptionally good value for money. The ultimate – not only in terms of the view – is the 45m² (485ft²) Deluxe Tower suite (from £58 via a booking website). There are also several beautiful, individually designed villas available; the Hobbit Villa is the cosiest. The Rambutan also has a restaurant and small spa and gym.

186 C4/5 Jl. Rambutan
0362 4 13 88; www.rambutan.org

Sawah Lovina £

The Sawah Lovina, a real oasis surrounded by lush tropical greenery, is also under Dutch management. If you come here from the heavily built-up beach area, you will find it hard to believe that you are in the same place. The Sawah is spacious, peaceful and attractive. The Balinese style bungalows in the well-kept gardens are large and in excellent condition. And, you can actually swim, and not just splash around, in the pool. To sum up – this is a very good deal. Insider Tip

186 C4/5 Jl. Mawar
0362 4 10 91;
www.sawah-lovina.com

Where to...
Eat and Drink

Prices
Expect to pay per person for a main course, excluding drinks and service:
£ under Rp60,000 **££** Rp60,000–120,000 **£££** over Rp120,000

LOVINA

Akar £

Insider Tip The vegan and vegetarian food served in this cute little café is so good that even meat lovers will ask for more. The dishes include the Lebanese-inspired Middle East Plate (with hummus and falafel) and a quiche with spinach, feta and caramelised onions. The smoothies and homemade ice cream are also delicious.

186 C4/5 Jl. Binaria
0362 3 43 56 36
Daily from 7am

Jasmine Kitchen £–££

If you need a little variety, then try this elegant restaurant with authentic Thai cuisine. The Som Tham papaya salad in particular will tickle the taste buds with its unusual flavours. But the curries and incomparable mango cheesecake are also fantastic.

186 C4/5 Jl. Binaria
0362 4 15 65
Daily 8am–10pm

Pasar Malam £

If you want to eat well (and cheaply) and are not too concerned about ambience, you should head to Kalibukbuk's night market, which is open every evening. Finish off your meal with *pisang goreng* (fried bananas) for dessert.

186 C4/5
Corner Jl. Raya Singaraja/Jl. Damai
Daily from 5pm

Rikki's Beach Bistro £–££
Sit on the beach drawing patterns in the sand with your toes as you sip an inexpensive cocktail and listen to soft live music (6pm–7pm) and watch the sun sink into the sea – ah yes, holidays are great! The menu is international and at lunchtime they mainly serve salads.
186 C4/5
Lilin Lovina Beach Hotel, Jl. Raya Singaraja
0362 4 16 70; www.rikkisonthebeach.com
Daily 1pm–10pm

Secret Garden £–££
Tastefully landscaped garden restaurant with just a handful of tables for a candlelight dinner of extremely tasty Balinese home cooking. And for dessert, they serve the Austrian speciality *Kaiserschmarrn* (shredded pancakes with raisins). Since it is not easy to find the restaurant you should use their free shuttle service, just give them a call.
187 D5 **Jl. Pura Dalem**
0887 3 32 10 07; www.secret-garden-restaurant.biz
Daily 5pm–10pm

The Damai £££
Those who want to treat themselves (and have packed more than just beach clothes) should dine in this luxury resort in north Bali. The drive through the green jungle and rice fields of Lovina's hinterland is the evening's first delight. And, the five-star oasis of good taste almost tops this with a restaurant that has a panoramic view of the coast. The service is perfect and the menu offers a three-course dinner (changed daily) of "royal" Balinese-French cuisine. The food is so good that it is often featured in cookery books and lifestyle magazines. All of the ingredients used are organic and come from the resort's own farm. Reservations essential.
186 C4/5 **Jl. Damai**
0362 4 10 08; www.thedamai.com
Daily noon–2pm and 5pm–9pm

Where to... Go Out

DANAU & GUNUNG BATUR

Here, everything revolves around the volcano. Guides are mandatory on the climbs (► 169) and are included in organised Batur tours. The cheapest option is to book directly with the **Association of Gunung Batur Trekking Guides**, which has an office at the end of the lakeside road in Toya Bungkah (► 136). They charge Rp400,000 per person for the tour (incl. a light breakfast). The summit is often shrouded in clouds in the late morning, and the climb usually starts at around 3am so that the group can reach the summit in time to see the sun rise. Remember to take drinking water, a pocket torch, sturdy shoes and some warm, waterproof clothing.

MUNDUK

Dozens of waterfalls cascade down into the valley in the area surrounding Munduk; all of the lodgings here have descriptions of the various trails and hand-drawn maps available for their guests. Organised hikes are also on offer as many of the waterfalls are impossible to find without knowledge of the local terrain. Non-guests of the **Puri Lumbung Cottages** (► 147) can also join the four full-day guided hikes that they organise. This also applies to their five mountain bike tours, the daily yoga classes, cooking and weaving lessons and all the other activities on offer at this eco-lodge. The **Bali Vespa Tour** (► 142) operators have numerous tours that combine hikes in the area surrounding Munduk and if you are looking for an adventure on four wheels, you then try one of

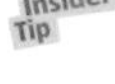

the extreme tours and expeditions organised by **Munduk Wilderness** (tel: 0812 38 12 14 44; www.mundukwilderness.com).

LOVINA

Dolphin safaris are the town's top attraction (► 141). Prices start at US$60 or Rp750,000 per person, depending on whether you book through your accommodation, a travel agency or onsite from the boatmen (who look for passengers on the beach in the late afternoon). Sometimes, they ask as much as Rp500,000 per person, so Insider Tip you must bargain in order to avoid overpaying. A snorkelling or fishing trip can be included in the deal if negotiated – it makes sense because you will be out at the reef.

Lovina itself is not much of dive site as the coral reefs have been destroyed by a combination of coral bleaching and fishing by using explosive blasts. So the local dive centres offer guided dive trips (ca. US$60–80) further afield. The dive centre with the best equipment is the **Spice Beach Club** (Jl. Raya Singaraja; tel: 0851 00 01 26 66; www.spicebeachclubbali.com), which offers dive safaris and PADI courses (US$320).

Lovina is the only place in north Bali where there is any kind of nightlife, usually in the tourist area in the centre of Kalibukbuk. However, you should not expect to find clubs and discos like those in Kuta. Here, most of the action takes place in pubs and bars, one of them will have some live music (after 9pm) and the music is more conducive for chilling, and is never deafeningly loud. The lights generally go out before midnight, occasionally later during the high season, or on special party nights.

Kantin 21 Lovina

Outdoor bar on the main road, which is a nightly meeting place for the youth of Lovina, and backpackers who like listening to rock and guitar music. It is cheap, and there is live music from 9pm (at the latest).

186 C4/5 Jl. Raya Singaraja
0812 4 60 77 91 Daily 1pm–2am

Poco Bar

Typical music bar where you can hang out, enjoy a cold draught beer and listen to live music.

186 C4/5 Jl. Binaria
0362 4 14 35 Daily 11am–1am

Spice Beach Club

The place to see and be seen. An elegantly styled lounge bar around a snazzy pool area offers creative fusion cuisine, good live music (from 9pm), shishas (Rp150,000) and imaginative cocktails (Rp40,000–150,000). There is a full moon party every month.

186 C4/5
Jl. Raya Singaraja 0851 00 01 26 66; www.spicebeachclubbali.com
Daily 9am–1am

The Duke

The Duke has perhaps the best music in Lovina. It is certainly *the* meeting place for expats and tourists over the age of 40. Music starts after 9pm and each night is different. Monday is Blues, Tuesday is Classics, Wednesday is Special Night, Thursday is Soul, Friday is Swing/jazz and on weekend it is a mix of everything.

186 C4/5 Jl. Mawar
0813 37 08 43 18; www.theoldies-lovina.com/lovina.htm
Daily 6pm–1am

Zigiz

Cosy bar with relaxed live acoustic music with a touch of reggae. Good place to make contacts, have a laid-back evening and enjoy the very inexpensive cocktails (there are more than 100 to choose from and most only cost Rp35,000–40,000).

186 C4/5 Jl. Binaria 0857 38 44 60 86; www.zigiz-bar.com Daily 1pm–1am

The West

Protection for an Endangered Species

At Proyek Penyu (www.reefseenbali.com) in **Pemuteran** (➤ 158) the focus is on the conservation of sea turtles – well worth a visit!

Not Just a Surf Mecca

About 10km (6mi) east of the **Pura Rambut Siwi** (➤ 160) is the rocky Pantai Medewi beach, a surfing hotspot.

Bird Paradise

A boat excursion from **Labuhan Lalang** (➤ 157) to the mangroves southwest of Pulau Menjangan is a real treat, not only for bird lovers.

Getting Your Bearings

The western tip of Bali, which stretches west of an imaginary line drawn from the Pura Tanah Lot in the south, to Lovina in the north towards Java, is by far the least-developed, most sparsely populated part of the island and also the one least likely to visited by tourists. Almost half of the area is protected and forms part of the Taman Nasional Bali Barat.

Until the 1930s, the Bali tiger – which is now extinct – used to prowl through the thickets of this very mountainous hide-away. Today, the national park's land-scape contrasts make is one of a kind; the 800km² (300mi²) area also includes Bali's top underwater attrac-tion, the coral gardens near the island of Pulau Menjangan in the extreme northwest of Bali. They are among the most spectac-ular coral reefs in Southeast Asia. As there is no accommodation on the island itself, Pemuteran, a small fishing village on the mainland, has developed into an alternative holiday resort that now not only attracts divers and snorkellers but also tourists in search of rest and relaxation by the seaside.

Just like on the southwest coast, where the beaches are still mostly pristine with sand, gravel and pebbles and stretch for miles along the ocean, this area is no longer only the domain of surfers. If you drive from here into the hinterland you will be able to follow babbling brooks lined with dense bamboo, and see colourful towers of fruit stacked along the roadside.

The traditional water buffalo races at Negara cannot be much fun for such gentle animals

Banyupoh
Grokgak
Brombong
Gunung Musi
1224 m
Taman Nasional Bali Barat 40
Bilukpoh
Gunung Patas
1580 m
1080 m
Sumbul
0 5 km
0 3 mi
Medewi
Satang
Tista
Sembung
Manggis Sari
Yeh Embang
Rambut Siwi
Medewi
Pulukan
Pulukan
Yuwuk Manis
Pura Rambut Siwi 43
Airsatang
Pekutatan
Pangiyangan
Yeh Leh
Badingkayu
Pangyangan
Gumbrih
Lumbung Kauh
Surabratan
Balian 44

TOP 10

At Your Leisure

Two Perfect Days

Start by travelling along the south coast, parallel to Bali's only national park, to the western tip of the island, where Java seems close enough to touch. Then you do a detour trip to the neighbouring island of Pulau Menjagan, which is a popular diving and snorkelling destination. You should schedule at least two days to travel to the most important destinations in west Bali. A rental car – with or without a driver – is essential for this tour.

Day 1

Morning

Start the day by driving to **44 Balian** (➤ 161), a holiday centre that has made a name for itself among tourists looking for peace and quiet, as well as surfers. You will not find any restaurants and cafés catering to tourists until you reach your destination at the end of the day and it is therefore a good idea to have a second breakfast here before heading on towards **43 Pura Rambut Siwi** (➤ 160).

Afternoon & Evening

It is hard to tell how long the trip to **42 Negara** (➤ 159) will take; it all depends on the traffic. It is only worth stopping if a water buffalo race is taking place. And the only reason for going 33km (20mi) to the **40 Taman Nasional Bali Barat** (➤ 158; below) is to take part in a guided hike near Cecik. The road turns off to the northwest of Bali in Cecik (straight ahead, it leads to Gilimanuk, the harbour for the ferries to Java). After 13km (8mi), you pass Labuhan Lalang (➤ 156), the harbour for trips to Pulau Menjangan. For the following 15km (9.5mi), as far as the holiday town of **41 Pemuteran** (➤ 158), the route is lined with dozens of hotels and resorts; you will be able to choose a place to have dinner from among the many restaurants in Pemuteran.

Day 2

Morning

9 **Pulau Menjangan** (➤ 156; above) is a wonderful place to enjoy the water: anybody who visits the west of Bali simply has to take a boat excursion to this island. You can decide whether you want to relax on the beach, go snorkelling or take the big plunge and dive into the depths. It is a good idea to take a lunch packet for your midday meal, which you can have made up in the harbour at Labuhan Lalang.

Afternoon & Evening

Go the whole hog – most visitors stay on Pulau Menjangan until the afternoon. The **Bali Tower Resto** (➤ 163), is an excellent choice for a late lunch. But the view from this restaurant, high above the ground, is even more impressive at sunset – if you are not too hungry and can wait, it is a better idea to have dinner here.

9 Pulau Menjangan

If you want to go diving off the coast of Bali, then Bali Barat National Park is far and away the best destination. Even at a depth of 40m (130ft), the crystal clear waters mean that you will have full views of the magical marine world. The tiny island – 1.8km (1mi) long and 3.5km (2mi) wide – is famed for its deep drop-offs and steep banks.

The drop-offs here plunge down as far as 60m (200ft) and the great variety of coral is equally spectacular. When Jacques Cousteau made an inventory in 1963, he counted more hard and soft corals in Pulau Menjangan than in the entire Caribbean. And today, even after coral bleaching – that has not spared Pulau Menjangan – most of the reefs around the island are still dense with growth and largely intact, and offer a protected and unbelievably beautiful habitat for countless creatures and plants (image ➤ 155).

Divers will see sights such as a large colony of garden eels, a great diversity of gorgonian sea fans, scorpion fish and batfish, ghost pipefish and seahorses, flatheads and groupers. Not to mention the Napoleon wrasse and lion fish, the eagle rays and frogfish, barracudas and sharks and more than one hundred other species of fish. During the rainy season you may even get to see manta rays and whale sharks and lots of turtles swimming by.

Pulau Menjangan is a paradise for divers and snorkellers

Exceptional Diving and Snorkelling

Not only are there steep walls for scuba divers to explore, but there are also sandy slopes and platform reefs, caves, steep overhangs and lagoon sites, as well as a 19th-century shipwreck at a depth of 40m (130ft). The conditions for divers and snorkellers are excellent. After the crossing from Labuhan Lalang, which takes around 30 minutes, you can get into the water directly at the pier in the south of the island and swim out to the reef edge, which is only about 20m–40m (65ft–130ft) offshore and where the visibility is 20–30m (65ft–100ft).

Menjangan means "deer" and the name refers to the wild Sunda samba or Java deer that swim over to the island

Another advantage is that there are no significant currents so you can float along the reef in peace surrounded by schools of fish.

TAKING A BREAK

Pulau Menjangan is a protected area and there are no restaurants there. You can have a lunch packet prepared at the *warung* near the dock in **Labuhan Lalang**. However, after you return from the island, a meal in the **Bali Tower Resto** (➤ 163) near the jetty, is a must. Insider Tip

184 B5

INSIDER INFO

- Companies offering diving and snorkelling trips to Pulau Menjangan can be found in all of the holiday resorts. However, the transfers are very time-consuming – for example, it is about a 6/7-hour drive from Kuta – and it is therefore a good idea to look for accommodation in **Pemuteran** (➤ 158) about 17km (10mi) away where there are several dive centres that either operate independently or are affiliated with the resorts. The services offered in Pemuteran are all more or less identical, with all the trimmings snorkelling trips by boat cost about Rp550,000 (half day, minimum of 4 participants) and two dives Rp1.5 million, while a private dive guide costs and addition ca. Rp500,000.
- As an alternative to Pemuteran, you can spend the night in **Labuhan Lalang**, which is also the point of departure for the boats. However, all of the accommodation offered here is extremely luxurious and it will be hard to find anything for less than £260 a night.
- Pulau Menjangan is part of the Bali Barat National Park so there is a **national park fee** of Rp225,000 for divers or Rp215,000 for snorkellers.
- In order not to stress the coral reef excessively, dive numbers are regulated and only a **limited number of divers** are admitted on a single day – it is therefore a very good idea to reserve your dives as early as possible.

- **Rules:** Feeding the fish and damaging the coral is strictly prohibited and it should be just as obvious that you should not walk on the reef with your fins in the shallow sections.

At Your Leisure

40 Taman Nasional Bali Barat

This area was designated a national park in 1983, it began as a nature park established by the Dutch, and is the only one of its kind on Bali. With an overall area of around 780km² (300mi²), it covers half of west Bali and almost 15% of the island. However – in spite of what you often read – it is not an "untamed jungle wildness" but rather a dry savannah with extensive monsoon and dense mangrove forests and only small isolated enclaves of rainforest. The reserve is best known for its extraordinary **variety of bird species**; it is believed to be home to more than 200 species. These include the endangered Bali starling – the national park was actually established to protect this bird. Increased deforestation, as well as the illegal animal trade, has threatened it with extinction; the last official reserve census in 2004 only recorded 37 specimens of the Bali starling. The Bali tiger is now extinct – it was last seen here in 1937 – and wild cattle, leopards and civet cats, in all probability, only exist on paper nowadays.

Only underwater does the flora and fauna meet the standards one expects from a national park – namely at the island of Pulau Menjangan (► 156), which is also within the reserve. The park headquarters, near Cekik south of Gilimanuk, organises **hikes** through the pristine nature; they are not particularly spectacular but will be rewarding for birdwatchers. A mandatory guide costs Rp100,000 (not included in the admission fee for the park). The visitors' centre especially recommends the two-hour **Tegal Bunder Trail** (easy hike, especially for bird watching) and the **Gunung Klatakan Trail**, a 5/6-hour hike through the rainforest.

185 D/E3

Bali Barat National Park Office Headquarter

Jl. Raya Cekik-Gilimanuk-Jembrana-Bali, Cekik

0365 6 10 60, tnbb@telkom.net

Daily 7:30am–5pm

Rp200,000

41 Pemuteran

Along with Candidasa, Amed and Lovina, Pemuteran is one of Bali's comparatively smaller and quieter tourist destinations. It lies on both sides of the main road, in the extreme northwest of Bali. All of

In Bali's northwest, the Bali Barat National Park stretches all the way down to the coast

Pemuteran is ideal for families as it is a relatively quiet holiday idyll with dark sandy beaches and calm waters

the beaches here are relatively narrow with fine dark sand and coarse gravel. The sea is usually glassy with excellent conditions for snorkelling. All the more so since 2000 when a **coral reforestation** project was introduced and corals were induced to grow on artificial reefs with gentle currents. The Biorock Project is the largest and most successful of its kind worldwide and was awarded a special United Nations prize. To see what such an artificial reef looks like, you just have to swim a short way out to sea from the Taman Sari Hotel. Here you can snorkel in water that is no more than 15m (50ft) deep and see around 500 steel structures that are so densely covered with corals that their original form is entirely overgrown.

If you want to see even more of the underwater world, you can take part in a snorkelling or dive tour to the nearby island of Pulau Menjangan (➤ 156), or if you prefer to stay on land, you can do a bicycle excursion. Most of the places providing accommodation in Pemuteran also have cooking and yoga courses available.

184 C4

42 Negara

Negara is the largest city in west Bali (30,000 residents) but there is very little of interest for tourists and it is usually just a transit place for most of the year. However, foreigners and the locals come together here between July and October when the *makepung*, traditional **water buffalo races** (image ➤ 153), are held. This is when

This small shrine on the beach at the Pura Rambut Siwi will be surrounded by water at high tide

the local farmers (who originally came from Java) ask the gods to bless their rice harvest.

The specially bred water buffalo are decked out for the occasion and the *cikars* – the chariots the animals pull – are richly decorated and painted in bright colours. They reach speeds of 50–60km/h (30–37mph). However, the winner is not the first to cross the finishing line but rather judged overall on the appearance of the buffalo, chariots and "jockey". The colourful and photogenic festival attracts not only tourists but also thousands of Balinese from all over the island.

The highlights of the racing season are the two derbies held on the 2km (1.2mi) long racetrack in **Mertha Sari** south of Negara. The first is the **Bupati Cup**, held on the Sunday before 17 August (Independence Day) and the second, the **Gubenur Cup**, which is held on changing dates in September or October and sometimes even broadcast on Balinese television. Between these two top events there are also other races held between July and September, they take place twice a month, usually on a Sunday.

184 C2

Jembrana Government Tourism Office

Jl. Dr. Setia Budi 1, Negara

0365 4 10 60

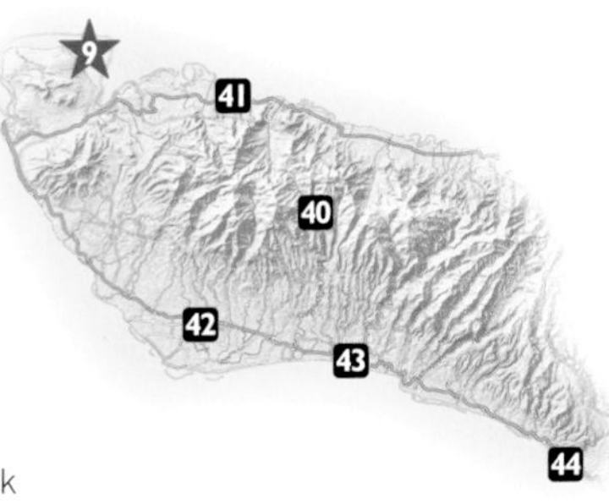

43 Pura Rambut Siwi

The beach village of **Pantai Medewi**, about halfway between Balian and Negara, is only of interest to avid surfers. But, 7km (4.5mi) further on, a 500m (1,600ft) access road leads to the magnificent Pura Rambut Siwi temple, on a high cliff above the raging sea. There is

ENOUGH CASH?
There are no ATMs or bureau de change in Balian – if you are short of cash, you will have to drive 30–40 minutes to the ATM in Tabanan.

a stairway that leads down to the beach and another one up to the sanctuary. This temple is one of the three most important sea temples in Bali, along with Pura Tanah Lot (➤48) and Pura Luhur Ulu Watu (➤50). It is as beautiful as its sister temples and the panoramic view is just as spectacular – but it is rarely visited by tourists.

185 E2
Daily 8am–5pm
Rp15,000, additional donation requested

44 Balian

Beach tourism on Bali means that there is a constant search for alternatives to the holiday resorts in the south. The tourism world has now discovered Balian, a 70km (44mi) long stretch of beach to the west of Kuta. Until a few years ago it was only well known to the locals. It is almost 40km (25mi) away from the nearest town of Tabanan. The grey sand beach, on either side of the mouth of the Balian River, is long, wide and perfect for long walks. Insider Tip The only problem is that it is not very good for swimming as the surf and waves that roll in along this coast can be wild and the currents are often very strong. That is why the area is popular with surfers and bodysurfers, and most of the tourists to this area are surfers. The raised road that runs parallel to the beach has a handful of restaurants and cafés, which all offer fine sea views, and you can mingle with the locals at the small *warungs* and at the market held every night in the village of **Lalang Lingah** 1km (0.6mi) away.

On the way to Balian, stop off at the **Museum Subak** in Tabanan for some insights into the work of the rice farmers.

186 B1

Museum Subak
Jl. Gatot Subroto
Mon–Thu and Sat 8am–4:30pm, Fri until noon

The view from the dunes down to the beach in Balian, which is especially popular with surfers

Where to... Stay?

Prices
Expect to pay per double room per night:
£ under Rp750,000 **££** Rp750,000–1.5 million **£££** over Rp1.5 million

There is no shortage of luxury resorts in Balian but further inland there are also some inexpensive bungalows. You get great value for money in Pemuteran, where the main road separates the budget accommodation on the land side from the more expensive ones on the beach side.

BALIAN

Gajah Mina Beach Resort £££
This luxurious resort high above the sea has private villas that satisfy the most discerning guests – and some have breathtaking views of the sea and the small, private sandy cove. There are pavilions where you can relax in the lush garden, which is also adorned with some stone statues. There is a restaurant and spa and yoga retreats are organised several times a year.
186 B1 **Jl. Pantai Balian**
0812 3 88 24 38; www.gajahminaresort.com

Gubug Balian Beach Bungalow £
This complex is located in the second row behind the beach. The two-storey stone bungalows have two large air-conditioned rooms with tiled floors and simple furnishing. Large swimming pool.
186 B1 **Jl. Pantai Balian**
0812 39 63 06 05, gubugbalian@gmail.com

Pondok Pisces/Balian Riverside Sanctuary £–£££
While the Pondok Pisces has exotic grass-roofed bungalows and rooms by the sea, the beautiful Balian Riverside Sanctuary bungalows are a few metres inland on the banks of the river. They are set in a lush green garden and all of the bungalows are comfortably equipped for two to six guests; some have a kitchenette, all have a fan (no air-conditioning). There is a swimming pool and Tom's Restaurant.
186 B1 **Jl. Pantai Bailan**
0852 37 83 98 99; www.pondokpiscesbali.com

Pondok Pitaya ££–£££
Located in a prime position, just behind the beach, the majority of the guests at this resort are Australian and a lot of beer is consumed in the evenings in the adjoining bar. There are rooms and bungalows in different sizes and price categories. Before you sign in you should ask to see the accommodation – some of the rooms/bungalows are not worth the money.
186 B1 **Jl. Pantai Balian**
0819 99 84 90 54; www.pondokpitaya.com

Shankari's Bali Retreat £–£££
This spiritual hideaway is about a 10-minute walk away from the beach. The bungalows are made of natural materials and are simply furnished with a bed and desk, fan, bath and balcony and have a view of the gardens and three swimming pools. The restaurant serves very reasonably priced Indonesian cuisine and a few classic Italian dishes. There is a

spa with massages and Balinese treatments and there are frequent yoga courses. Cheaper if you reserve via a bookings website.
186 B1 Jl. Raya Gilimanuk
0361 81 49 93; www.shankaribalivilla.com

PEMUTERAN

Adi Assri Beach Resort ££–£££
Pale walls, wood finishes, marble floors, four-poster beds and air conditioning – and that is in the lowest category bungalow (there are five price categories), while the most expensive villa even has a private pool. The complex includes a well-kept garden, a large swimming pool, a dive centre and a spa.
184 C4 Jl. Singaraja-Gilimanuk
0362 9 48 38;
www.adiassribeachresorts.com

Kubuku Eco Lodge £
The Kubuku is about a 10-minute walk away from the beach and this means that you can stay in one of the 14 bright and airy, relatively comfortable, rooms for as little as £18 a night. A good restaurant, attractive pool and wide range of activities – even volcano climbs on Java – are on offer, in addition to yoga retreats, bicycle tours, bird watching and much, much more.
184 C4 Jl. Singaraja-Gilimanuk
0813 38 57 53 84; www.kubukuhotel.com

Taruna Homestay £–££
Homestay is not a correct description for this beach resort. You will not come into contact with the family here but will experience a level of service comparable to a four-star hotel. The garden and swimming pool seem to be straight out of a painting, the restaurant serves excellent food and the bright and airy rooms offer considerable luxury for relatively little money. You will feel immediately at home. In addition to the dive trips to Pulau Menjangan offered everywhere in Pemuteran, the Taruna organises (expensive) trekking tours in the national park and sightseeing tours to Java.

Insider Tip

184 C4 Jl. Singaraja-Gilimanuk
0813 38 53 63 18;
www.tarunapemuteran.com

Tirta Sari Bungalows £–££
Enchanting, small oceanfront resort: the neat bungalows are nestled in a pretty garden area with a fantastic swimming pool. Pleasant restaurant, professional spa, friendly service and wide range of activities.
184 C4 Jl. Singaraja-Gilimanuk
0877 62 13 21 23;
www.tirtasaribungalows.com

Where to...
Eat and Drink

Prices
Expect to pay per person for a main course, excluding drinks and service:
£ under Rp60,000 **££** Rp60,000–120,000 **£££** over Rp120,000

LABUHAN LALANG

Bali Tower Resto £££
This restaurant, which is also known as Menjangan Tower, is part of The Menjangan resort. It is located inside a 33m (108ft) wooden tower and has spectacular 360° panoramic views over the national park as far as Pulau Menjangan from

the fourth and fifth floor viewing platforms. Enjoy the view while you dine on Mediterranean and Indonesian gourmet cuisine.
184 B4 The Menjangan
0362 9 47 00; www.themenjangan.com
Daily 7:30am–11pm

BALIAN

Secret Bay Restaurant £££

The only outstanding restaurant in Balian is part of the Gajah Mina Beach Resort (► 162). It has an absolutely unique location under the palms above beautiful Secret Bay. Insider Tip Even waiting for your dinner is a pleasure, as you can relax on comfortable loungers, listen to gentle jazz and sip one of their unusual cocktails. And the meals served – creations of exquisite fusion cuisine – make the evening absolutely perfect.
186 B1 Jl. Pantai Balian
0812 3 88 24 38; www.gajahminaresort.com

PEMUTERAN

Bali Balance Café & Bistro ££

This leafy garden restaurant, on the main road hillside, serves the best coffee and tastiest baked goodies in Pemuteran. Sit under white umbrellas while you enjoy your food and drink, and you'll feel that the prices – similar to what you would pay back home – are quite justified.
184 C4 Jl. Singaraja-Gilimanuk
0853 37 45 54 54; www.bali-balance.com
Daily 8am–6pm

Frangipani Restaurant & Bar

This restaurant, which is set back from the main road, is on the second floor and overlooks Pemuteran. Pleasant atmosphere, attentive service and a wide range of Indonesian and European dishes on the menu. Most of the prices are a little higher than usual (this also applies to the vast selection of cocktails).
184 C4 Jl. Arjuna 0813 38 41 86 68;
www.frangipanirestaurant.com
Daily 1pm–10pm

La Casa Kita

There are no "Balinese pizzas" here, instead the pizzas are made in a wood-burning oven and are really crispy, have perfect toppings and are not too expensive.
184 C4 Jl. Singaraja-Gilimanuk
0852 38 89 02 53 Daily 11am–11pm

Where to... Go Out

Laidback west Bali has little or no nightlife to speak of. This area attracts those looking to spend their days surfing (Balian) or snorkelling or diving (off the coast at Pemuteran and Pulau Menjangan).

PEMUTERAN

There are now around 25 dive centres in Pemuteran and if you include the ones in Labuhan Lalang and surroundings the number is closer to 40. All of them vie for their piece of the dive-tourism pie. The offers are usually very similar and the equipment is almost always well maintained. You will be in good hands at one of the **Werner Lau international dive centres**; there are two in Pemuteran, one in the Matahari Resort and one in the Pondok Sari Resort. Bookings can be made online at www.wernerlau.com or by telephone at the individual dive centres (tel: 0812 3 85 91 61). PADI diving courses cost £285, diving trips to Pulau Menjangan £70, snorkelling trips £38 and dives starting at the beach in Pemuteran £20. It is also possible to book diving packages including accommodation.

Walks & Tours

1 CLIMBING UP GUNUNG AGUNG

Hike

DURATION: 8/12/14 hours (return)
ALTITUDE DIFFERENCE: 1,400/1,600/2,100m (4,600ft/5,250ft/6,900ft)
START/END: For the south route, the Pura Pasar Agung 189 D2, for the west route, the Pura Besakih 188 C2

This active stratovolcano's enormous cone dominates the entire eastern part of the island. A hike up to the summit of this, the highest 3,142m (10,308ft) and most sacred mountain on Bali, provides the perfect balance after a few lazy beach days. However, this is only really an option if you are in Bali during the dry season from April to September (the best time is July or August), are in really good physical shape, and have the appropriate gear (sturdy hiking boots and warm, waterproof clothing). As a rule, the tour guides provide everything else, such as pocket torches, trekking poles, gloves and provisions. And you should be sure to only set out with an experienced guide as the route is hard to find, steep, slippery and sometimes dangerous!

Sunrise over Gunung Agung – an unforgettable moment

1–2 West Route

There are three routes to the summit of the "great mountain" (the meaning of Gunung Agung). The most difficult and longest by far is the **West** or **Besakih Route**. It starts at the upper east end of the Besakih Temple. The ascent usually begins at around 11pm because the Gunung Agung is often enveloped in clouds in the morning. This start time means you will reach the summit in time to watch the sunrise and – with a little bit of luck – to see the unbelievably spectacular 360° views.

The path ascends more than 2,100m (6,900ft) along the steep

MOUNTAIN GUIDES

You can find experienced local guides in Tirtagangga (► 109), in front of the Pura Besakih (► 104) and at the Mahagiri Restaurant (► 108). In addition, almost all of the travel offices in the holiday resorts offer tours to the crater and summit of Gunung Agung. However, the most qualified mountain guides can be found in Selat near the starting point of the southern route to the summit. We recommend **Dartha Mount Agung Trekking** (tel: 0852 37 00 85 13, agungguide@yahoo.com; www.darthamountagungtrekking.com). An all-inclusive organised tour costs around Rp1–1.5 million for two people; you can also book your accommodation on site, as well as a transfer from or to the holiday resorts. Insider Tip

At the top! On a clear day the view from Gunung Agung extends as far as Bali's neighbouring islands

western flank of the Agung. At first it passes through dense mountain rainforest. After around six hours you will reach the **Kori Agung** rock face at an altitude of 2,500m (8,200ft) and then enter the steep lava fields of the summit region.

2–3 West Route

After another two to three sweaty hours you will finally reach the **summit**. This is actually the highest rim of the **volcano crater**, which is about 700m (2,300ft) across. Its steep inner walls, which are usually

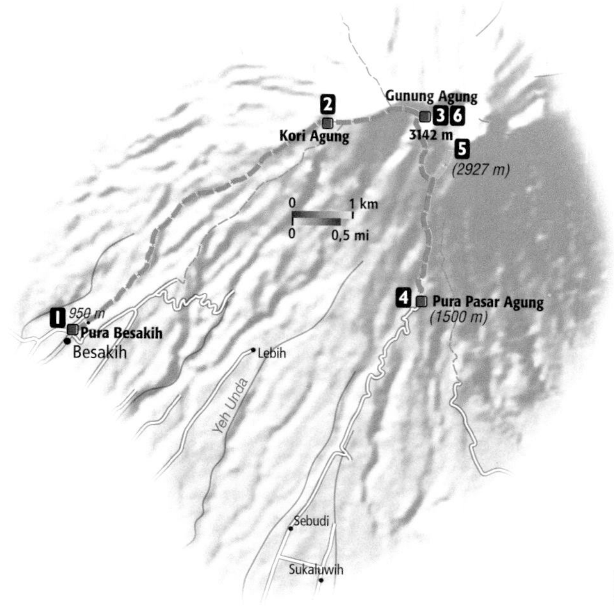

> **MOUNT AGUNG CAMPING TOUR**
> Having to get up in the middle of the night – or maybe not even going to bed – to climb the steep and slippery paths up the volcano in the dim light of pocket torches to Gunung Agung's summit is possibly not everybody's idea of hiking pleasure. One solution to this is the two-day **Mount Agung Camping and Spiritual Meditation Tour** organised by Dartha Mount Agung Trekking (➤ 166). It follows the southern route over two days (overnight in tents) so you have plenty of time to admire the landscape (and to meditate).

covered with clouds of sulphur, plunge down as far as 200m (650ft).

3–1 West Route

The descent is at least as difficult as the ascent and it will take a good seven hours before you get to **Pura Besakih,** the final goal of this gruelling, but all the more memorable hike.

4–5 South Route

The two **south routes** start and end at the **Pura Pasar Agung** temple at an altitude of around 1,500m (5,000ft) on the southern flank of the volcano. It is about 10km (6mi) north of Selat by car. As with the western route, the morning clouds make it necessary to set out early in order to reach the top before sunrise. The start is usually around midnight for those who want to reach the actual summit or at 2am if the tour ends at the crater rim.

This route is also steep and sometimes slippery but, all in all, easier to walk than the western route. The first section to the **crater rim** at 2,927m (9,603ft) should take about three to four hours.

5–3 South Route

The final ascent to the **summit** will take another one to two hours. The panoramic views from both destinations are uniquely beautiful. If you are not quite sure about how fit you really are, it would be best to take the shorter tour because about 40% of the tourists who set out to conquer the peak give up along the way!

South Routes 3–4

As with the west route, you will also need to manage your energy levels as the descent takes about the same time as the climb.

On the descent you have the entire eastern Bali at your feet

2 CLIMBING GUNUNG BATUR

Hike

DURATION: 4–6 hours (return)
ALTITUDE DIFFERENCE: ca. 600m (2,000ft)
START/END: Pura Jati 188 B3

Many people are really intrigued by bizarre volcanic landscapes, but even those who are not, will be impressed by the ascent of the 1,717m (5,633ft) Gunung Batur. Of course, climbing up over slopes covered with lava is not the easiest thing imaginable – and you might even regret heading out on the climb – but once you reach the top, and see the world at your feet and the red-golden sun rising, the effort involved in the climb is all quickly forgotten.

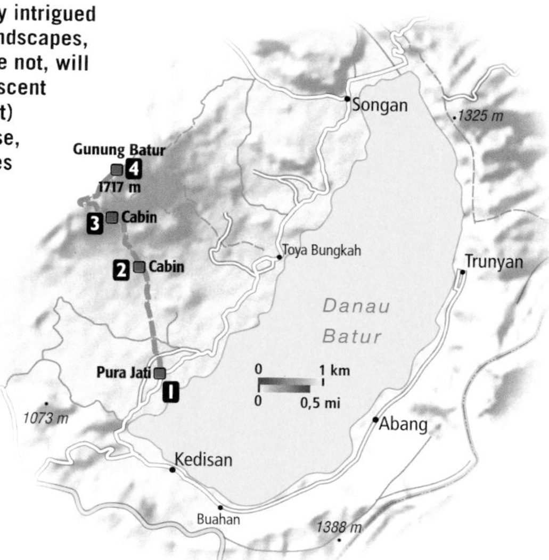

1–2

Three different routes lead from the Danau Batur to the summit of Gunung Batur. By far the shortest and easiest – and that it why it is the one the guides (➤ 149) usually choose – starts directly at the **lakeside road** in **Pura Jati**. This is also where you can park your car (take all of your valuables with you). And of course, the same applies here as it does to Gunung Agung – remember to take drinking water, a pocket torch, sturdy shoes and warm, waterproof clothing.

Despite the fact that the path is covered in thick layer of slag, so it feels as though you are walking in soft sand, and that you have make

Gunung Batur guides definitely do not have a fear of heights

The wonderful view from Gunung Batur over to its more formidable big sister, Gunung Agung

your way by torchlight, you will still make good progress. After about an hour, you will arrive at a **wooden hut** that serves as a kiosk (from 7am). This is usually the spot for your first brief rest.

2–3

On the next section you can take it easy for about 20 minutes before the path becomes steep and slippery – this is when those foolish enough to set out wearing trainers or normal shoes will bitterly regret that decision. You will have to use your hands to help you climb and you will definitely slip along this section. And then after about two hours, all of a sudden a square shadow appears in the diffuse light ahead, and you will have reached another wooden hut. This marks the end of the torture for almost all of the hikers because it is on the lower eastern **crater rim** at an altitude of about 1,500m (5,000ft) and high enough to be able to admire the sunrise and view over large parts of Bali, the Lombok Strait and all the way to Lombok itself. The caldera is also accessible from here – it hisses and whistles from countless fumaroles – some sections of the path are so warm that you can feel the heat through the soles of your shoes.

3–4

Very few still have enough energy to attempt the **summit** itself, although it is only 200m (650ft) higher up. The path is easy to find – it starts right at the hut and heads upwards as a narrow, exposed track left of the **crater rim**.

4–1

After arriving at the summit, you make your way around the upper crater and then back down over slag fields to the lower rim of the crater before finally arriving back at the **starting point**.

TAKING A BREAK

The rim of the crater is actually the destination of this hike and that is where the guide usually takes a couple of eggs out of his bag and cooks them in a hot spring before serving them, along with some bread and bananas, as a welcome breakfast. If you want something else, you will have to carry it yourself or be happy with the biscuits that are served at the **kiosks** along the way (only after about 7am).

3 IN THE SHADOW OF THE VOLCANOES

Tour

DISTANCE: ca. 350km (220mi)
TIME: 3 days
START: Ubud ✚ 191 E4

This route makes its way around both the 3,142m (10,308ft) sacred mountain of Gunung Agung, as well as the active Gunung Batur volcano. It crosses the highest pass on the island at an altitude of 1,640m (5,380ft) and combines the highlights of east Bali into a fascinating trip that can easily be extended by a few more days.

1–2

When you set out from **Ubud** (➤ 74) to make your way around the volcanically active centre of the island, you will discover that Bali is one massive blossoming garden. This fertile region of the island has been densely populated for centuries, and it is the agricultural heartland of Bali. It is entirely dominated by rice cultivation (➤ 20) right up to **Klungkung** (➤ 117), the capital of east Bali.

2–3

As you continue your journey, the impressive cone of Gunung Agung soon dominates the landscape. Driving through the expanse of green tropical forests, you can catch occasional glimpses of the views down to the coast, sections of which have black volcanic sand beaches. There are several holiday centres along the way, such as **Padang Bai** (➤ 111) and **Candi Dasa** (➤ 119), but some of the places away from the coast are even more beautiful. And, you should be sure to visit **Tenganan** (➤ 113) the fascinating traditional village of Bali's indigenous people.

3–4
The route continues on to **Tirtagangga** (➤ 109) where, under the shade of a banyan tree, there are some sacred springs that feed water into several natural basins – the perfect place for a refreshing dip in cool waters. For many visitors to Bali, Tirtagangga is possibly the most beautiful refuge of them all – the ideal place to spend a lazy day doing as little as possible.

4–5
Back on the main road, follow the Singaraja signposts and head through the dramatically beautiful landscapes of the rice terraces of Tirtagangga. As you leave them behind you – a few kilometres after **Tista** – the views change and are now dominated by blackish solidified lava. Gunung Agung, which you will now drive around, fits perfectly into this landscape, which is dotted with only few scattered cacti and some goats. This landscape stays unchanged for the next 70km (44mi) as you drive towards **Kubutambahan** always within sight of the sea and black sand beaches.

5–6
After leaving Kubutambahan, you follow the Kintamani signs to the southeast and then a further 36km (22mi) steeply uphill until you reach an altitude of 1,640m (5,380ft). When you reach the top you will be able to admire the fabulous panoramic view of the volcano and **Lake Batur** (➤ 132) before following the rim of the caldera, which has an impressive column of fire rising up its centre. It is now a matter of personal choice whether you spend the night on the shore of **Danau Batur** or on the rim of the crater in **Penelokan** (➤ 132).

6–7
Bangli (➤ 80) is barely 30km (18mi) away from Penelokan. Before you head for the Pura Kehen temple, you should visit the **Desa Tradisional Pengelipuran** (➤ 81) village.

7–8
From there you follow the **Ubud** signposts and head via **Pura Bukit Dharma** (➤ 91) and **Goa Gajah** (➤ 91) back to where this tour started.

DETOUR
Leave Kubutambahan and turn left off the main road and head towards the hinterland and the small village of **Jagaraga**. This village is well worth visiting to see the Pura Dalem (✚ 187 E5) temple decorations. They include a relief that depicts a battle between two historic aircraft and one of a vintage car (➤ image below).

4 GILI TRAWANGAN

Boat tour

DURATION: At least 2 days
START: Sanur 191 E2/3, Serangan 191 D2, Nusa Lembongan 192 A2/3, Padang Bai 192 B4 or Amed 189 E2

If your idea of paradise is an idyll of snow-white sandy beaches lapped by emerald waters with stretches of breathtakingly beautiful coral gardens then this small island (4km/2.5mi long and 2km/1.2mi wide) is for you. It is the largest and most enchanting of the three tiny islands off the coast of Lombok that make up the Gili Islands.

Divided Worlds

No matter where about on Bali you travel from, the fast boat to Gili Trawangan is a highlight in itself, as it will afford you some breathtaking views of the gigantic volcano cones on Bali and Lombok. The two islands are separated by the Lombok Strait (35km/22mi wide and 3,000m/ 9,800ft deep), which marks a biogeographic dividing line for flora and fauna. The animal and plant world on the western side have Asian characteristics while the eastern side is Australian – a fact resulting from the geological past of the Indonesian archipelago. In addition, the Lombok Strait – the biogeographic Wallace Line – also differentiates the areas peoples (the Malayan type is dominant to the west and the Melanesian to the east). And, last but not least, it also forms a climate divide between the tropical monsoon zone in the west and the relatively dry zone in the east.

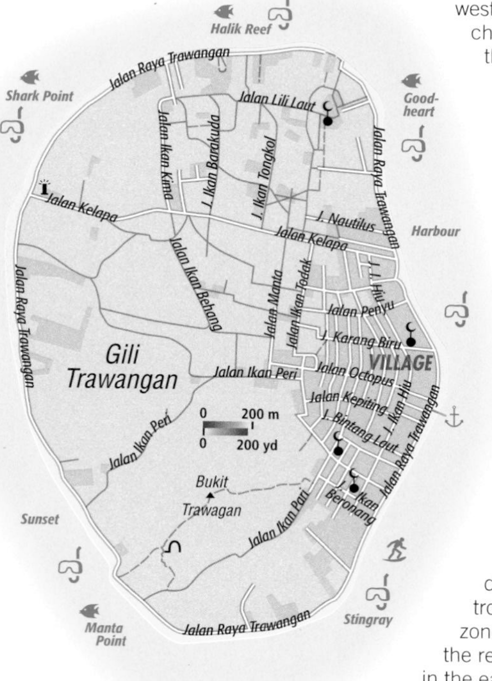

Holiday dreams become a reality on the tiny island of Gili Trawangan

South Sea Dream and Dive Paradise

Although there is no clear-cut dividing line, Bali and Lombok and, of course, the tiny **coral island lined with palm trees**, Gili Trawangan – the Gili Island with the most developed tourist infrastructure – are worlds apart. The island offers everything that you could possibly want from a beach holiday in the South Seas. The only drawback is that it can be difficult to find peace and quiet during the high season from June to late August. Gili Trawangan is Indonesia's version of Thailand's Ko Pha Ngan – the party island for young (and young-at-heart) tourists. And if you are passionate about snorkelling and/or diving, an excursion to this island is a must. The marine world around Trawangan is full of exotic wonders and sometimes all you have to do is dip your mask under water to see them – that's how shallow and crystal clear the water is.

INSIDER INFO

- The **crossing** with the fast boat from Padang Bai, or Amed, to Gili Trawangan takes about one hour, 90 minutes from Nusa Lembongan and about two and a half hours from Sanur and Serangan near Denpasar, where there are the most connections. The one-way fare, including the transfer from your lodgings in south Bali, costs around Rp500,000–600,000. The website www.gilibookings.com provides an overview of all the connections and you can also you can also book your crossing via the website – this should be done at least one day in advance of your departure date.
- In contrast to Bali, with its Hindu population, most of the people living on Trawangan are Muslims. This means that **topless** bathing is taboo and wearing **beachwear** away from the beach is also frowned upon.
- All kinds of **drugs** are offered rather openly on Gili Trawangan; some restaurants even have magic mushrooms on the menu. Nevertheless, they are illegal and drug offences are met with severe penalties – and no exceptions are made for tourists.
- The **currents** between the islands can be extremely strong and those who attempt to swim from Gili Trawangan to Gili Meno, which is only around 800m (2,600ft) away, are risking life and limb.

Practicalities

BEFORE YOU GO

WHAT YOU NEED

● Required
○ Suggested
▲ Not required

	UK	USA	Canada	Australia	Ireland
Passport (must be valid for at least six months beyond your date of entry)	●	●	●	●	●
Visa (for a stay that is not longer than 30 days, ➤ 32)	▲	▲	▲	▲	▲
Onward or Return Ticket	●	●	●	●	●
Health Inoculations (Tetanus, Measles/Rubella/Mumps, Hepatitis A/B)	○	○	○	○	○
Travel Insurance Policy (➤ 180)	●	●	●	●	●
Driver's Licence (international)	●	●	●	●	●
Credit card (as a security deposit)	○	○	○	○	○

WHEN TO GO

Denpasar

High season / Low season

JAN	FEB	MAR	APRIL	MAY	JUNE	JULY	AUG	SEP	OCT	NOV	DEC
31°C	31°C	31°C	31°C	31°C	30°C	29°C	29°C	30°C	31°C	32°C	31°C
88°F	88°F	88°F	88°F	88°F	86°F	84°F	84°F	86°F	88°F	90°F	88°F
Sun	Sun	Sun	Sun	Sunshine and showers	Sunshine and showers	Sunshine and showers	Sunshine and showers	Sunshine and showers	Sunshine and showers	Sun	Sun

Sun   Sunshine and showers

The temperatures listed above are the **average daily maximum** for each month in Denpasar. Bali is in the tropical belt and is influenced by the monsoon winds that give the island its two seasons. The **southeast monsoon** that blows from early or mid-May until September brings the dry season; the driest and coolest months are July and August when temperatures regularly exceed 26 °C (79°F) in the south and it only rains three or four days a month. From October to April/May the **west monsoon** blows and brings with it the rainy season with frequent, heavy downpours – especially south of the central mountain range (maximum in December and January). However, it usually rains mainly in the afternoon and at night and there are many days of constant sunshine. The temperatures are highest during this period and the humidity can be extreme.

GETTING ADVANCE INFORMATION

- www.indonesia.travel/en
- www.bali.com
- www.thebalibible.com
- www.baliguide.com
- www.bali-paradise.com
- www.balitravelforum.com
- www.bali-travel-online.com
- www.balidiscovery.com
- www.balinews.com

GETTING THERE

By Air There is no shortage of international flights to Bali's Ngurah Rai International Airport (IATA Code: DPS). Due to the runway restrictions at Bali's airport there are no direct flights from the UK, Europe or North America but there are connections through many major Asian hubs that then fly nonstop to Bali.

From the UK and Europe International flights operated by airlines such as British Airways, KLM, Singapore Airlines (in cooperation with Lufthansa), Qatar Airways, Cathay Pacific, Malaysia Airlines and Emirates all involve a connecting flight from an airport in the Middle East or Asia.

From Australia and New Zealand Qantas and Virgin Australia serve Bali direct from several Australia cities and there are direct flights to Bali with Air New Zealand.

From the US & Canada The best connections are through the major Asian hubs or via Europe. The number of transfers and the flight time depends on which city you depart from.

TIME

Bali is in the **Central Indonesian Time Zone** (WIT). There is no daylight saving time in Indonesia and the difference to Greenwich Mean Time (GMT) is +8 in winter and +7 in summer

CURRENCY & FOREIGN EXCHANGE

Currency The Indonesian currency is the rupiah (Rp). Coins are issued in denominations of Rp50, Rp100, Rp500 and Rp1,000 and banknotes in Rp1,000, Rp5,000, Rp10,000, Rp20,000, Rp50,000 and Rp100,000.

Exchange rates In recent years, the exchange rate has remained relatively stable at £1 = Rp16,000–17,000; you can check the current rate at www.oanda.com.

Currency exchange The exchange rates are generally better in Indonesia than at your local bank. There are banks in all the major cities but the tourist centres also have facilities for changing foreign currencies and travellers cheques – often at a better rate.

Cash You can withdraw cash from the ATMs in the holiday centres and cities, as well as in many smaller towns. They accept all the standard credit and debit cards. In case of an emergency, it is a good idea to have some cash with you (this can also be in euros or US dollars; low denominations and make sure that the banknotes are not creased).

Credit Cards The popular credit cards are widely accepted in the tourist centres; a credit card is essential for booking tickets and for other online services.

ON BALI

Bali Tourism Board
Jl. Raya Puputan 41
Renon, Denpasar
☎ 0361 23 56 00
www.balitourismboard.org

Practicalities

WHEN YOU ARE THERE

NATIONAL HOLIDAYS

1 January: New Year's Day; **March/April:** Good Friday, Easter; **21 April:** Kartini Day (Indonesia Women's Day; semi-official); **May:** Ascension Day; **17 August:** Independence Day; **1 June:** Pancasila Day (Five Principles of the State; semi-official); **5 October:** Indonesian National Armed Forces Day; **25 Decenber:** Christmas Day

In addition to these public holidays, which are celebrated throughout Indonesia, Bali also has some **flexible public holiday** dates.

ELECTRICITY

The power supply is 230 volts AC (50 Hz) and the sockets take two-pronged plugs. Visitors from countries that use 220/240 volts will need to bring a converter and adaptor. There are frequent power failures and voltage fluctuations during the rainy season.

OPENING HOURS

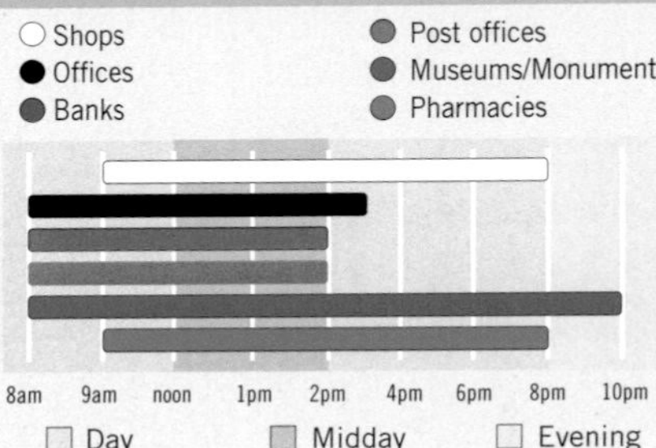

The Balinese attitude towards timekeeping is described as *jam karet* (meaning "**elastic time**") so while there is an official time, it is of little importance. The **temples** frequently visited by tourists do have set opening hours. The **shops and businesses** in the holiday centres open/close one or two hours later than usual.

ETIQUETTE

You should only visit sacred sites in modest dress (trousers for men) with your shoulders covered. Visiting a temple with an open wound (this also includes menstruation) desecrates the sanctuary and is taboo. The left hand is believed to be unclean and you should never present or accept anything with your left hand. Kissing and public displays of affection are considered to be improper. Nude/topless bathing is not allowed. Avoid gesticulating wildly when you speak, avoid talking/standing with your hands on your hips and never point at other people.

TIPS/GRATUITIES

Tips are not expected in restaurants but you can give ca. 10% or a maximum of Rp15,000 if you are very satisfied with the service. The same applies to taxis. The drivers of rental cars and guides should be tipped at least Rp50,000 a day for their services.

TIME DIFFERENCES

Bali (WIT)
12 noon

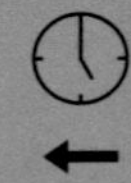

London (GMT)
5am

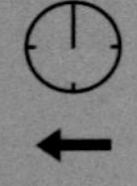

New York (EST)
midnight

Los Angeles (PST)
9pm

Sydney (AEST)
3am

STAYING IN TOUCH

Post Stamps can be purchased in the *kantor pos*, or post office, and there is one in every town or village. In the tourist centres you can also buy them in the kiosks and souvenir shops. Indonesian post boxes are red. Postcards and letters to Europe normally take five to ten days and are sent *per udara* (airmail).

Public Telephones The cheapest places to make calls are internet cafés (using Skype, for instance) and telephone exchanges (*wartel*); the cheapest tariffs start with the access numbers 01017 and 01013. Calls made from hotels are the most expensive. Making landline calls in Bali can be quite frustrating as the network is often overloaded. In many places there are telephones that use prepaid phone cards; the cards are available in post offices, supermarkets and hotels. Mobile telephone numbers always begin with 08.

International Dialling Codes

Dial 00 followed by:

UK:	**44**
USA / Canada:	**1**
Irish Republic:	**353**
Australia:	**61**
New Zealand:	**64**
Indonesia:	**62**

Mobile providers and services The network coverage is good/excellent everywhere on the island but the roaming fees can be high. It is usually cheaper to buy a prepaid SIM card once you arrive in Bali. They are available from XL-Data (www.xl.co.id/en) and other providers and only cost a few rupiahs. National calls will then cost ca. Rp500/per minute, international calls to Europe ca. Rp5,000/min. and SMS ca. Rp3,000. A 3G flat rate is available from ca. Rp5,000 (35 MB/1 day) and a monthly flat rate (2.3 GB) from Rp200,000.

WiFi & Internet WiFi hotspots are widespread in the holiday resorts; guests can log in free of charge in almost all restaurants, cafés, pubs, etc., and hotels and accommodation places also offer free internet access.

PERSONAL SAFETY

Violent crime against tourists is rare. However, it is always best to take the usual precautions:

- Never leave your luggage or valuables unattended and keep your jewellery and other valuables in the hotel safe. Lock your door at night or when you are out of your room.
- Don't carry around large quantities of cash.
- Always be aware of your surroundings and keep your eye on your drink in discos and bars, as drinks are sometimes spiked.
- Never get into a taxi alone at night in (or around) Kuta and avoid dark backstreets.
  In an emergency, contact the Tourist Police in Kuta (tel: 0361 22 41 11).
- Be very careful when you swim in the sea, especially on the south coast and around Kuta. The currents are extremely strong and every year there are drowning victims.
- Only very experienced motorcyclists should risk the Balinese traffic. The "unconventional" style of driving, and narrow streets, frequently prove to be deadly for tourists.

EMERGENCY	**112**
POLICE	**110**
FIRE BRIGADE	**113**
RESCUE SERVICE	**151, 111, 115**
AMBULANCE	**118**

HEALTH

Insurance It is essential that you take out a travel insurance policy that covers medical and dental treatment, and the cost of transport back home in the case of an emergency.

Medical Services Only the holiday centres in Bali have international standards of medical care. And, only there will you be able to find English-speaking doctors who can be contacted through your hotel or travel agent. Your diplomatic mission, the hotels and/or tour operators also have a list of recommended doctors and hospitals in Bali. Bear in mind that many will not meet international standards and in the case of an emergency, you should try to be flown out to Singapore or back home as soon as possible.

Weather The sun near the equator really packs a punch. A sun hat and sun-protective clothing, as well as a high SPF sunscreen are essential. You should avoid physical exertion during the first days while you adjust to the tropical climate.

Medication & Inoculation The **pharmacies** (Indonesian: *apotik* or *toko bat*) are usually well stocked but if you take prescribed medication, bring them with you, plus a copy of your prescription, in case you need to refill it while in Bali. Many medicines can be purchased without a prescription and are cheaper than what you would pay back home. Tourists arriving from some countries may require yellow fever vaccinations. Consult your travel agent or your government's health department for specific recommendations. They may advise on tetanus, polio, diphtheria or hepatitis A/B shots. The malaria risk in Bali is low and, as a rule, no prophylaxis is necessary.

Safe Water Tap water in Bali is not safe to drink. Bottled water (check that it is sealed) is available everywhere and is very cheap. The ice cubes in the tourist centres are usually safe but should be avoided in the rural areas.

TRAVELLING WITH A DISABILITY

There are no special facilities for people with disabilities in Bali. **Bali Access Travel** (tel: 0851 00 51 99 02; www.baliaccesstravel.com) specialises in travel for the handicapped and offers a variety of services.

CHILDREN

Children are welcomed with open arms everywhere in Bali. Special attractions for children are marked out in this book using the logo shown above.

RESTROOMS

The condition of the public toilets (Rp2,000; usually squat toilets) is appalling. During the day, you should use the WCs in restaurants and cafés. Toilet paper is rare and you should always have some with you.

CUSTOMS REGULATIONS

Importing souvenirs made from internationally endangered plants and animals (such as ivory, reptile leather, tortoiseshell or coral) on the CITES list is illegal.

EMBASSIES & CONSULATES

UK (Denpasar)
☎ 0361 27 06 01

USA (Denpasar)
☎ 0361 23 36 05

Ireland (Jakarta)
☎ 021 28 09 43 00

Australia (Denpasar)
☎ 0361 2 00 01 00

Canada (Jakarta)
☎ 021 25 50 78 00
(or contact the Australian embassy in Denpasar)

Useful Words and Phrases

In contrast to many other Asian languages, Europeans find Indonesia's national language Bahasa Indonesia (or "Bahasa" for short) relative easy to learn. It is closely related to Malay. There are very few plurals, which are usually formed by doubling the singular (*bulan* = month; *bulan-bulan* = months). However, a doubled word can also have a completely different meaning. There are no articles in the language. In Bahasa, "What does the room cost?" is translated as *Berapa harga kamar kosong ini?* (or "How much cost room?"). The conjugation of verbs is done away with, and verbs also have no tenses and retain their original form in the sentence.

There are some special aspects in connection with the pronunciation of Bahasa. A "c" is invariably pronounced as "tsch" ("Candi" = "Tschandi"); the letter "j" at the beginning of a word is spoken as "dsch" ("Jalan" = "Dschalan") and a "z" is always silent (= ts).

When starting a conversation, it is polite to ask where somebody comes from or his or her name (*Siapa namayana?*). And it is also polite to ask a question about their health (*Apa khabar?)* and the reply is usually *bagus, bagus* ("good, good") or *khabar baik* ("I feel good").

USEFUL PHRASES

Yes/No **Ya/Tidak**
Maybe **Mungkin/Bis jada/Barangkali**
Please (offer/invitation) **Silankan**
Please (asking for help) **Tolong**
You're welcome **Kembali**
Thank you **Terima kasih**
Thank you very much **Terima kasih banyak**
Please (don't mention it) **Sama-sama**
Excuse me, please **Maaf!/Sorry!**
Pardon? **Maaf, bagaimana?**
I don't understand **Saya tidak mengerti**
I only speak a little... **Saya hanya bisa berbicara sedikit...**
Do you speak... **Apa Bapak/Ibu/kamu berbicara bahasa...**
...English? **...Inggris?**
...French? **...Perancis?**
Could you help me please? **Apa Basak/ Ibu bisa menolong saya?**
I would like to... **Saya mau...**
I (don't) like this **Saya (kurang) menyukainya.**
Have you got...? **Apa di sini ada...?**
How much is it? **Berapa harganya?**
What time is it? **Jam berapa sekarang?**

GREETINGS, FAREWELL

Good morning **Selamat pagi!**
Good afternoon (until 3pm) **Selamat siang!**
Good afternoon (until 6pm) **Selamat sore!**
Good evening **Selamat malam!**
Hello **Halo!**
My name is... **Nama saya...**
What is your name? **Siapa nama Bapak/Ibu?**
How are you? **Apa kabar Pak/Ibu?**
Thank you. And you? **Terima kasih. Dan Bapak./Ibu/kamu?**
Goodbye **Sampai jumpa lagi!**
Good night **Selamat tidurr!**
See you **Permisi!/Ayo!/Bye!/Daag!/Mari!**
See you **Sampai nanti!**
See you tomorrow **Sampai besok!**

DIRECTIONS & GETTING AROUND

left/right **kiri/kanan**
straight ahead **terus, lurus**
close/far **dekat/jauh**
Please, where is...?/where are...? **Maaf, di mana...?**
How far is it to the...? **Berapa jauhnya ke...?**
Which bus goes to...? **Bus mana pergi ke...?**
Where can I buy a ticket? **Di mana saya bisa membeli karcis?**
Where is the next taxi rank? **Di mana pangkalan taksi terdekat?**
To the train station/...hotel **Ke stasiun/hotel.**
To...please **Ke...**
Where is the nearest petrol/gas station? **Di man pompa bensin terdekat?**
I would like...litres **Saya mau...liter**
...regular petrol **...premium**
...super **...premix**
...diesel **...solar**
...mix **...bensin campur**
Fill up the tank, please **Isi penuh!**

Useful Words and Phrases

BREAKDOWN

Help! **Tolong!**
Attention! **Awas!**
Watch out! **Hati-hati!**
Please urgently call **Tolong cepat panggil**
...an ambulance **...ambulans**
...the police **...polisi**
...the fire brigade **...pemadam kebakaran**
It was my/your fault **Ini kesalahan saya/ Bapak/Ibu**
Please give me your name and address **Tolong berikan saya nama dan alamat Bapak/Ibu**

FOOD & DRINK, SHOPPING

Where can I find **Di mana ada**
...a good restaurant? **...restoran yang baik?**
...a typical restaurant? **...restoran yang khas?**
Could you please book a table for tonight for four **Saya mau memesan meja untuk empat orang untuk malam ini.**
Do you have vegetarian meals/diet food? **Apa ada hidangan tanpa daging/untuk diet?**
Could we have more rice/water, please? **Apa bisa mendapat nasi/ar lagi?**
Enjoy your meal! **Selamat makan!**
Not too spicey, please **Tolong jangan terlalu pedas!**
May I have the bill, please? **Saya mau bayar!**
The meal was excellent **Makanannya enak sekali.**
This is for you **Ini untuk Bapak./Ibu.**
Where is the toilet? **Di man kamar kecil?**
Where can I find... **Di mana saya bisa membeli**
...a pharmacy? **...apotik?**
...a bakery? **...toko roti?**
...a department store? **...pasar swalayan?**
...a travel agency? **...biro perjalanan?**
Where can I find a bank/bureau de change? **Di mana ada bank/money changer di sini?**
I'd like to change...pounds into rupiahs **Saya mau menukar...Pound dalam Rupiah**

ACCOMMODATION

I have a room reservation **Saya telah memesan kamar die sini**
Do you have a room available... **Apa di sini masih ada kamar kosong...**
...for one night? **...untuk satu malam?**
...for one week? **...untuk satu minggu?**
...with a bath? **...denang kamar mandi?**
How much per night... **Berapa harga kamar dengan...**
...including breakfast? **...makan pagi?**
...half board? **...makan pagi dan malam saja?**
...full board? **...tiga kali makan?**

HEALTH

Could you recommend a doctor please? **Apa Bapak/Ibu tahu seorang dokter yang baik?**
I have an upset stomach **Perut saya tidak enak.**
I have diarrhoea **Saya diare.**
I have a fever **Saya demam**
I have pain here **Saya sakit di sini**
The heat/food doesn't agree with me **Saya tidak tahan makanan itu/panas**

NUMBERS

0 **nol**
1 **satu**
2 **dua**
3 **tiga**
4 **empat**
5 **lima**
6 **enam**
7 **tujuh**
8 **delapan**
9 **sembilan**
10 **sepuluh**
11 **sebelas**
12 **dua belas**
13 **tiga belas**
14 **empat belas**
15 **lima belas**
16 **enam belas**
17 **tujuh belas**
18 **delapan belas**
19 **sembilan belas**
20 **dua puluh**
21 **dua puluh satu**
30 **tiga puluh**
40 **empat puluh**
50 **lima puluh**
60 **enam puluh**
70 **tujuh puluh**
80 **delapan puluh**
90 **sembilan puluh**
100 **seratus**
200 **dua ratus**
1,000 **seribu**
2,000 **dua ribu**
10,000 **sepuluh ribu**
½ **seperdua, setengah**
⅓ **sepertiga**
¼ **seperempat**

Road Atlas

For chapters: See inside front cover

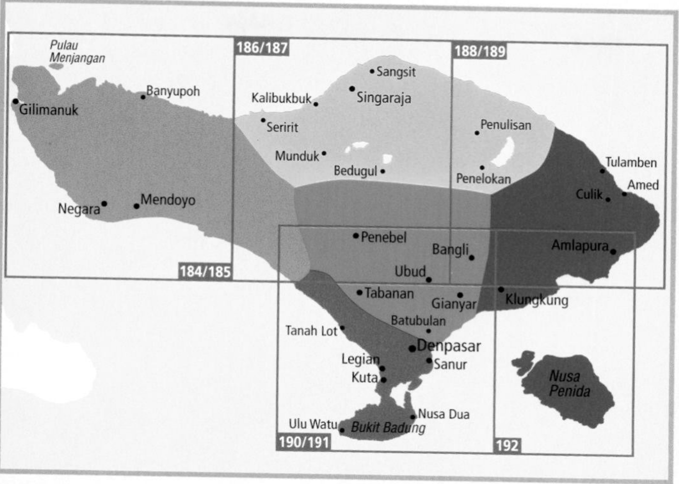

Key to Road Atlas

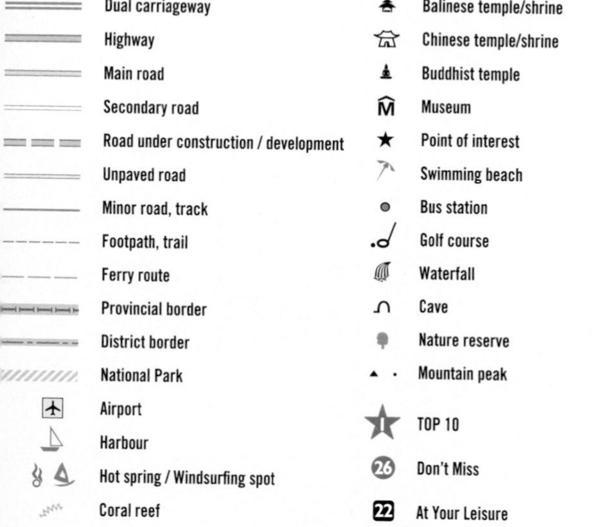

1 : 250.000

0 5 10 km

0 2.5 5 mi

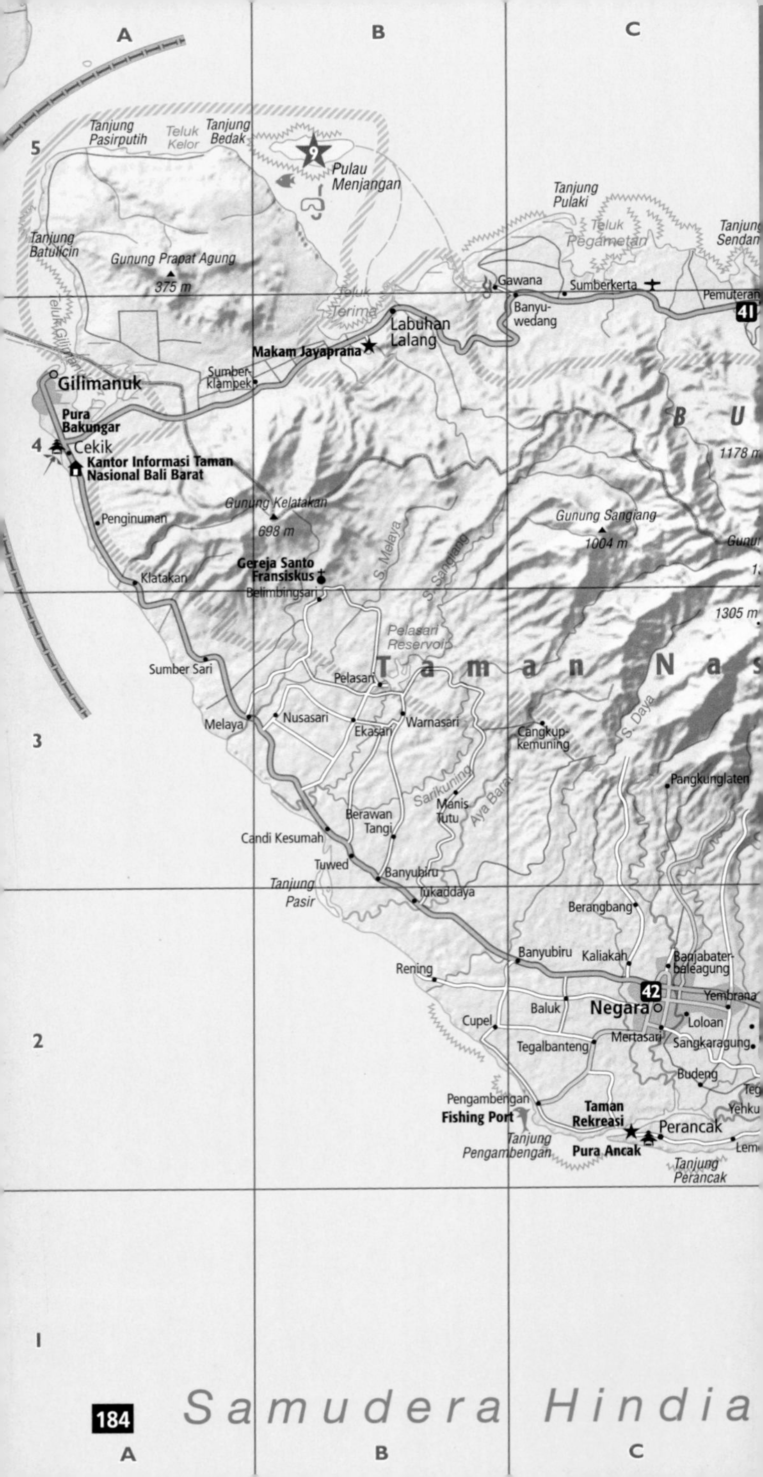
A
B
C
5
4
3
2
1
Tanjung Pasirputih
Teluk Kelor
Tanjung Bedak
9
Pulau Menjangan
Tanjung Pulaki
Teluk Pegametan
Tanjung Batulicin
Gunung Prapat Agung
375 m
Teluk Terima
Gawana
Sumberkerta
Pemuteran
41
Banyuwedang
Labuhan Lalang
Makam Jayaprana
Teluk Gilimanuk
Sumberklampek
Gilimanuk
Pura Bakungar
Cekik
Kantor Informasi Taman Nasional Bali Barat
1178 m
Gunung Kelatakan
698 m
Gunung Sangiang
1004 m
Penginuman
Gereja Santo Fransiskus
Klatakan
Belimbingsari
S. Melaya
S. Sangiang
1305 m
Pelasari Reservoir
Taman Nas
Sumber Sari
Pelasari
Melaya
Nusasari
Ekasari
Warnasari
Cangkupkemuning
S. Daya
Pangkunglaten
Sarikuning
Manis Tutu
Aya Barat
Berawan Tangi
Candi Kesumah
Tuwed
Banyubiru
Tanjung Pasir
Tukaddaya
Berangbang
Banyubiru
Kaliakah
Banjabaterbaleagung
Rening
42
Yembrana
Baluk
Negara
Cupel
Loloan
Mertasari
Sangkaragung
Tegalbanteng
Budeng
Pengambengan
Fishing Port
Taman Rekreasi
Perancak
Tanjung Pengambengan
Pura Ancak
Tanjung Perancak
Samudera Hindia

D
E
F
Laut Bali
5
4
3
2
1
Banyupoh
Tanjung Gondol
Pura Pulaki
S. Banyupoh
Gondol
Penyabangan
LELENG
Musi
Kayuputih
Grokgak
Tinga Tinga
Celukan-bawang
Brombong
Kalisada
Teluk Bawang
Tukadsumaga
Gunung Musi 1224 m
Gunung Merbuk
Gunung Mesehe 1344 m
40
sional Bali Barat
Bilukpoh
Gunung Patas 1580 m
JEMBRANA
Embang
Sumbul
Sekarkejula
Medewi
Pangkung Belangsah
Satang
Sebual
Pesantren
Sembung
Pangkung gondang
Mendoyo
Pencaringan
Yeh Embang Kauh
Nusamara
Sambul
Mendoyo-dagintukad
Tegal-cangkring
Rambut Siwi
Yeh Embang
Yeh Embang Kangin
Medewi
Pulukan
Asah
Dlodbrawah
Munduk
43
Pura Rambut Siwi
Airsumbul
Airsatang
Tinggi
Pekutatan
Medewi Beach
Pangyangan

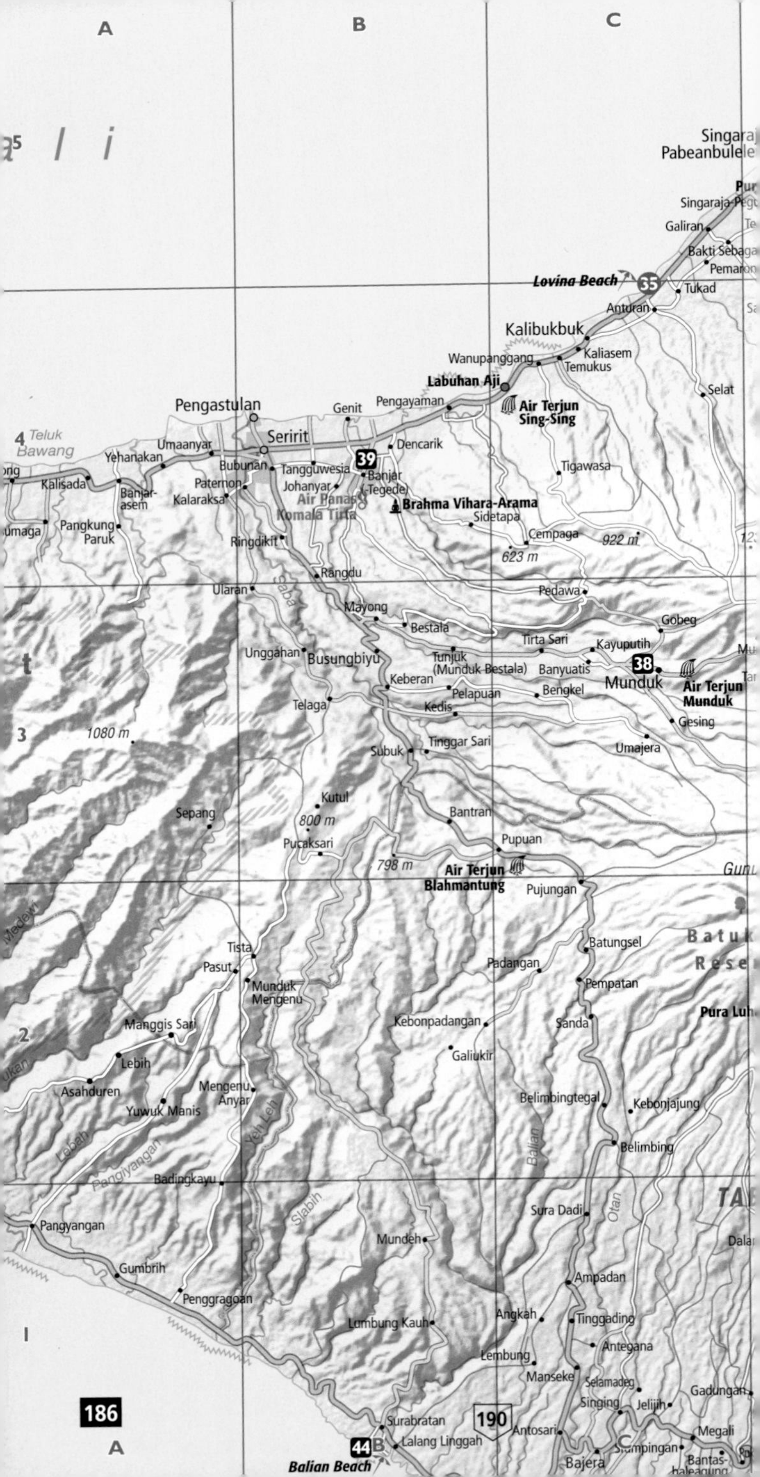
A
B
C
Bali
Singaraja
Pabeanbuleleng
Singaraja-Pegu
Galiran
Bakti Sebaga
Pemaron
Lovina Beach
35
Tukad
Anturan
Kalibukbuk
Kaliasem
Wanupanggang
Temukus
Labuhan Aji
Selat
Air Terjun Sing-Sing
Pengastulan
Genit
Pengayaman
Teluk Bawang
Seririt
Dencarik
Umaanyar
Yehanakan
Bubunan
39
Tangguwesia
Tigawasa
Kalisada
Paternon
Banjar (-Tegede)
Johanyar
Banjar-asem
Kalaraksa
Air Panas Komala Tirta
Brahma Vihara-Arama
Sidetapa
Pangkung Paruk
Cempaga
922 m
623 m
Ringdikit
Rangdu
Saba
Ularan
Pedawa
Mayong
Gobeg
Bestala
Tirta Sari
Kayuputih
Unggahan
Busungbiyu
Tunjuk (Munduk Bestala)
Banyuatis
38
Munduk
Air Terjun Munduk
Keberan
Pelapuan
Bengkel
Telaga
Kedis
Gesing
1080 m
Tinggar Sari
Subuk
Umajera
Kutul
Sepang
800 m
Bantran
Pucaksari
Pupuan
798 m
Air Terjun Blahmantung
Pujungan
Medewi
Batungsel
Tista
Padangan
Pasut
Munduk Mengenu
Pempatan
Kebonpadangan
Sanda
Manggis Sari
Galiukir
Lebih
Asahduren
Mengenu Anyar
Yuwuk Manis
Belimbingtegal
Kebonjajung
Yeh Leh
Lebah
Belimbing
Pangiyangan
Balian
Badingkayu
Slabih
Otan
Sura Dadi
Pangyangan
Mundeh
Gumbrih
Ampadan
Penggragoan
Angkah
Tinggading
Lumbung Kauh
Antegana
Lembung
Manseke
Selamadeg
Singing
Jelijih
Gadungan
Surabratan
190
Antosari
Megali
Lalang Linggah
44
Balian Beach
Bajera
Simpingan
Bantas-Baleagung
4
3
2
1

D
E
F
Tanjung Bunkulan
Pura Meduwe Karang
Sangsit-Babakansangsit
Pura Beji
Bungkulan
Kubutambahan
Air Sanih
Bukti
Tanjung Sanih
Pura Ponjok Batu
Bangkah
Pacung
Sangsit
Krabokan
Kloncing
Penarukan
Sinabun
Banyuning
Sinengdalem
Penglatan
Pura Dalem Jagaraga
Balian
Menyali
Bilabajang
Depaa
Sembiran
Pura Dalem
Gedung Kirtya
Singaraja
37
Suwug
Alasangkin
Petandakan
Sawan
Tamblang
Tangkid
Bontihing
Tetajun
Panci
Sambangan
Buleleng
Tenaon
Sudaji
Bebetin
Pakisan
Tegehe
Padangbulia
Silangayang
Sekumpul
Klandis
Satra
Penginyahan
Ambengan
Pegayaman
Galungan
1140 m
Kembangsari
Air Terjun Gitgit
Gitgit
36
1219 m
Lemukih
Dausa
1087 m
232 m
Tambakan
Lampu
Mabi
Belantih
1308 m
1255 m
Catur
Wanagiri
Gunung Catur 2098 m
Amerta Sari
Danau Buyan
34
1341 m
Mungsengan
Ayung
Asah Gobleg
Danau Tamblingan
Desa Pancasari
2020 m
Uliangunungban
Candi Kuning
Satu
Banjarlawak
Pura Gubug Tamblingan
1903 m
Danau Bratan
7
Pura Ulun Danu Bratan
Bukit Mungsu
Kebun Raya
Belok
Gunung Lesong
Tiingan
Manikaya
1860 m
Candi Kuning Dua
Bedugul
Tijingan
Mengani
Pelaga
Temantanda
Gunung Sangiyang 2093 m
Gunung Pohen 2069 m
Kiadan
Bunutin
Jeruklegi
Sidan
Batunye
Meyungan
Baturiti
Nungnung
Gunung Batukaru 2276 m
Tonjiwa
Puasan
944
Sandan
Pacung
Bangah
Gate
Sandakan
Penyabangan
Puakan
Angari
Tegeh
Gunungsari
Senganan-kanginan
Apuan
Pakuseba
Batukau
Pura Luhur Batukau
19
Jatiluih (Jati Luwih)
Senganan-kawan
Tundak
Taro
Pura Gunung Kawi
Bolangan
Peneng
Wongayagede
Pinga
Punggang
Semadi
Babahan
Buahan
Yehempas
Poyan
Petang
Payangan
Baru
Luwus
Palean
Pontang
Penganggaan
487
Pujung
Pemanis
Bluangan
Lebah
Pujungklod
Sandan
Tengkudak
Penebel
Pangsan
Sangketan
Caumarga
Kedisan
Getasan
Cacan
Kukup
Gadungen
Perean Tengah
Petiga
Pagending
Lebe
Melinggih
Tangkup
Penatahan
Bereteh
Basangba
Kelusa
Yehtengah
Tegallinggah
Carangsari
Bang
Celuk
Tegalalang
Yeh Panas
Keliki
Manuaba
Buruan
Cepik
Njelati
Babakan
Samuan
Taman Lembah
Grane
Jempeng
Tunjuk
Marga
Sapat
Pegubugan
Ngis
Sandan
Sembung
Pura Bukit Sari
Sebali
Beng
Caublayu
Selat
Kesiyut
Wanasari
Taman Kupu Kupu (Bali Butterfly Park)
Kekeran
Kedewatan
Petulu
Timpak
Sarosi
Mambal
Sangeh
24
Museum Neka
187
Blubuk
Bluahan
Panti
Monkey Forest
Lodpasar
Sayan
Batuaji
Rianggede
Museum Puri Lukisan
Sembunggede
Subamia
Calagi
Batannyuh
Ayunan
191
Pura Gunung Lebah
23

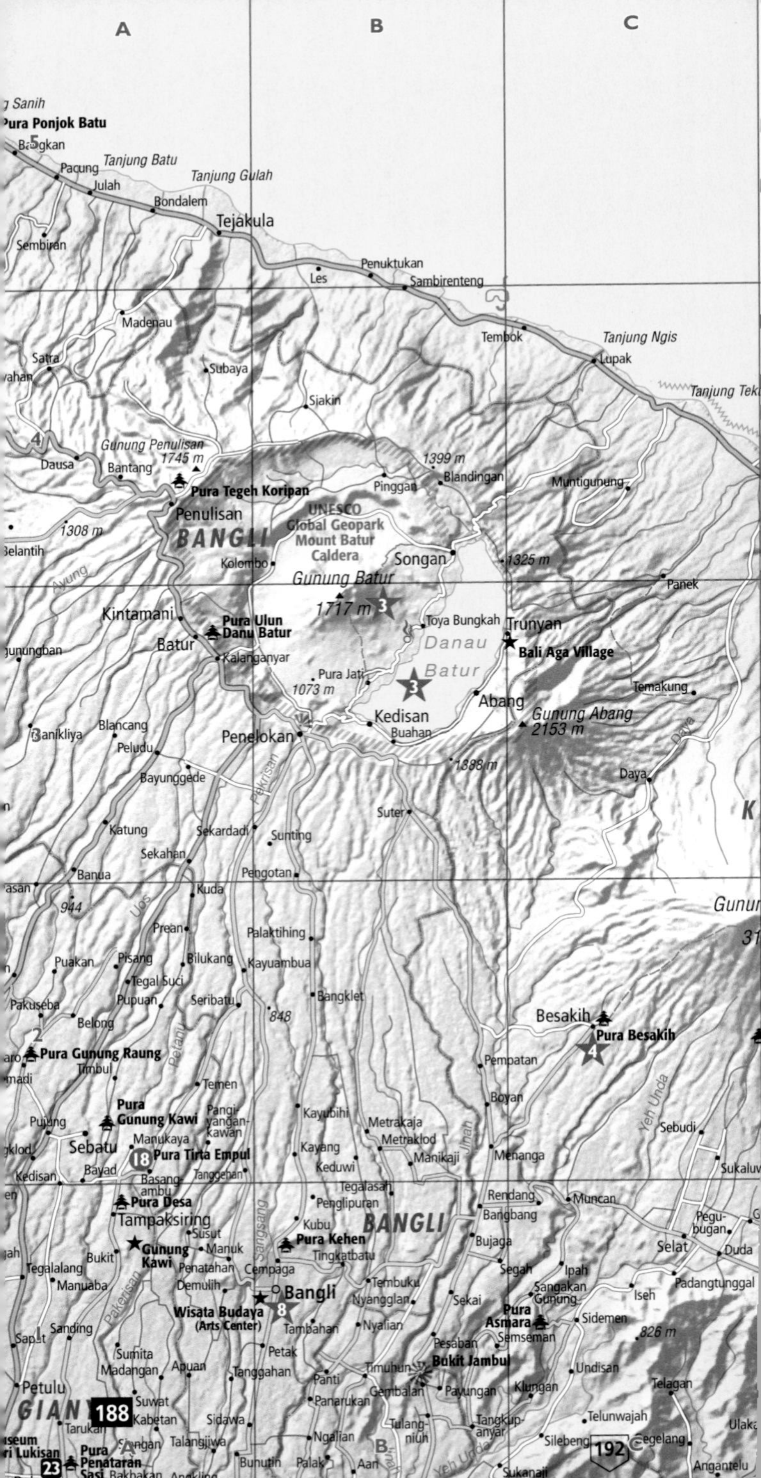
A
B
C
Pura Ponjok Batu
Pacung
Tanjung Batu
Tanjung Gulah
Julah
Bondalem
Tejakula
Sembiran
Penuktukan
Les
Sambirenteng
Madenau
Tembok
Tanjung Ngis
Lupak
Satra
Subaya
Sjakin
Tanjung Tek
Gunung Penulisan
1745 m
Dausa
Bantang
1399 m
Blandingan
Muntigunung
Pura Tegeh Koripan
Pinggan
Penulisan
UNESCO
Global Geopark
Mount Batur
Caldera
1308 m
BANGLI
Kolombo
Songan
1325 m
Gunung Batur
Panek
1717 m
Kintamani
Pura Ulun
Danu Batur
Toya Bungkah
Trunyan
Danau
Batur
Bali Aga Village
Batur
Kalanganyar
Pura Jati
1073 m
Temakung
Abang
Gunung Abang
2153 m
Kedisan
Buahan
Banikliya
Blancang
Peludu
Penelokan
1388 m
Daya
Bayunggede
Pakrisan
Suter
Katung
Sekardadi
Sunting
Sekahan
Banua
Pengotan
Kuda
944
Uos
Prean
Palaktihing
Puakan
Pisang
Bilukang
Kayuambua
Tegal Suci
Pupuan
Seribatu
848
Bangklet
Pakuseba
Belong
Besakih
Pura Besakih
Pura Gunung Raung
Timbul
Petanu
Pempatan
Temen
Yeh Unda
Boyan
Pura
Gunung Kawi
Pangi-
yangan-
kawan
Kayubihi
Metrakaja
Jinah
Sebudi
Pujung
Sebatu
Manukaya
Metraklod
Pura Tirta Empul
Kayang
Manikaji
Menanga
Kedisan
Bayad
Keduwi
Tanggehan
Basang-
ambu
Tegalasah
Rendang
Muncan
Pura Desa
Penglipuran
Bangbang
Tampaksiring
Kubu
BANGLI
Pegu-
bugan
Susut
Pura Kehen
Bujaga
Selat
Duda
Gunung
Kawi
Manuk
Sangsang
Tingkatbatu
Bukit
Tegalalang
Penatahan
Cempaga
Segah
Ipah
Manuaba
Demulih
Tembuku
Sangakan
Gunung
Padangtunggal
Bangli
Nyangglan
Sekai
Iseh
Wisata Budaya
(Arts Center)
Pura
Asmara
Sidemen
Pakerisan
Sanding
Tambahan
Nyalian
Semseman
826 m
Pesaban
Sumita
Petak
Madangan
Apuan
Tanggahan
Timuhun
Bukit Jambul
Undisan
Panti
Petulu
Gembalan
Payungan
Klungan
Telagan
Suwat
Panarukan
Kabetan
Sidawa
Tangkup-
anyar
Telunwajah
Tulang-
niuh
Tarukan
Ngalian
Silebeng
Gegelang
Ulaka
Pura
Penataran
Sasi
Talangjiwa
Yeh Unda
Bunutin
Palak
Aan
Angantelu
Bakbakan
Sukanaji
Pengkalanan

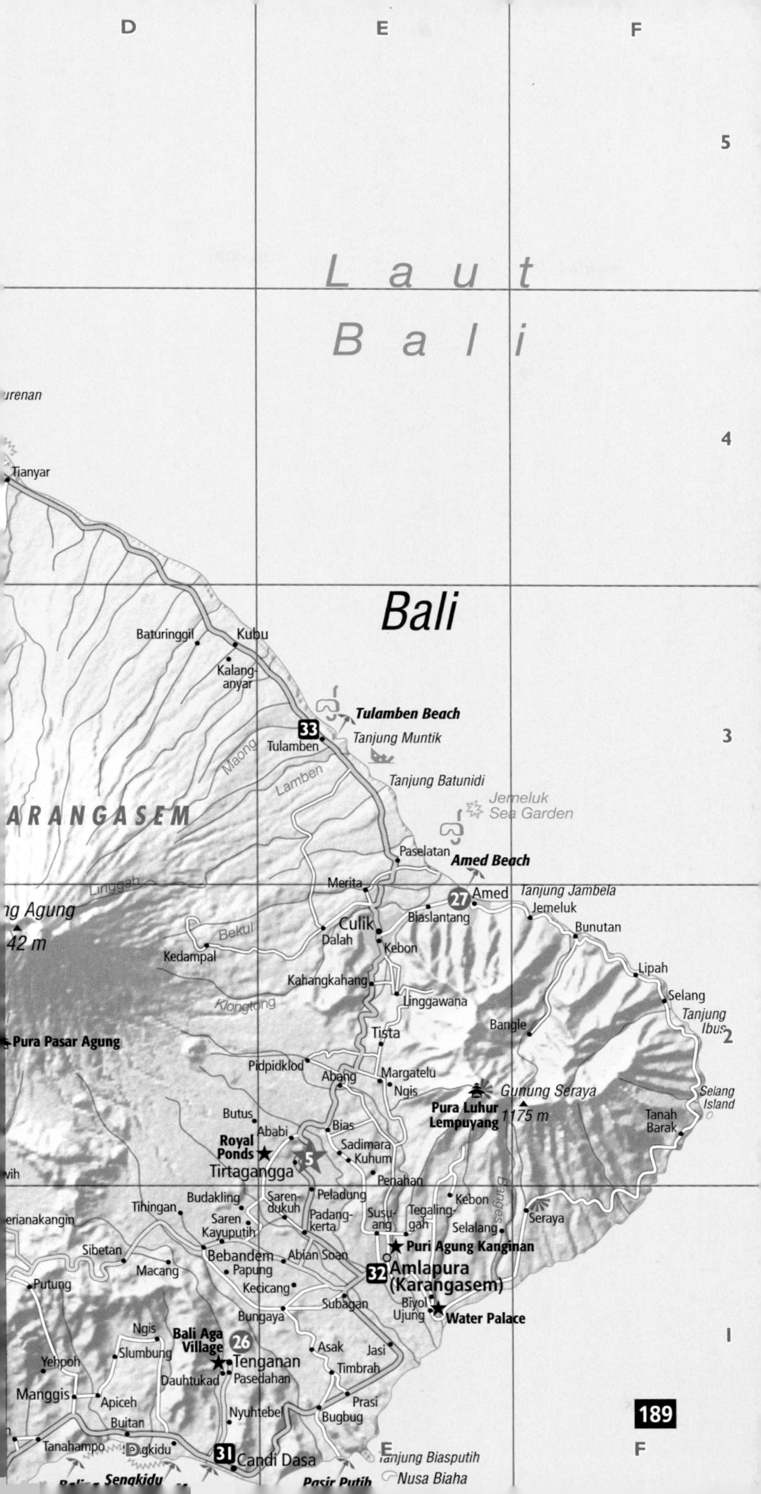
D
E
F
5
4
3
2
1
Laut Bali
Bali
urenan
Tianyar
Baturinggil
Kubu
Kalang-anyar
Tulamben Beach
33
Tulamben
Tanjung Muntik
Maong
Lamben
Tanjung Batunidi
Jemeluk Sea Garden
KARANGASEM
Paselatan
Amed Beach
Merita
27
Amed
Tanjung Jambela
Jemeluk
Biaslantang
Bunutan
Linggah
ng Agung
42 m
Bekul
Culik
Dalah
Kebon
Kedampal
Kahangkahang
Lipah
Selang
Linggawana
Tanjung Ibus
Klongtong
Bangle
Tista
Pura Pasar Agung
Pidpidklod
Abang
Margatelu
Ngis
Gunung Seraya
Pura Luhur Lempuyang
1175 m
Selang Island
Tanah Barak
Butus
Ababi
Bias
Royal Ponds
Sadimara
Kuhum
5
Tirtagangga
Penahan
Bangles
Kebon
Seraya
Budakling
Saren-dukuh
Peladung
Tihingan
Saren
Padang-kerta
Susu-ang
Tegaling-gah
Selalang
Kayuputih
Puri Agung Kanginan
Sibetan
Bebandem
Abian Soan
Macang
Papung
32
Amlapura (Karangasem)
Putung
Kecicang
Subagan
Biyol
Ujung
Water Palace
Bungaya
Ngis
Bali Aga Village
26
Asak
Jasi
Slumbung
Tenganan
Yehpoh
Pasedahan
Timbrah
Dauhtukad
Manggis
Apiceh
Prasi
Nyuhtebel
Buitan
Bugbug
Tanahampo
Ngkidu
31
Candi Dasa
Tanjung Biasputih
Nusa Biaha
Sengkidu
Pasir Putih

A
B
C
187
Penganggaan
Belimbing
Sandan
Tengkudak
Penebel
Pemanis
Sangketan
TABANAN
Cacan
Pagending
Sura Dadi
Otan
Mundeh
5
Penatahan
Dalang
Tegallinggah
Yeh Panas
Ampadan
Buruan
Cepik
Lumbung Kauh
Angkah
Tinggading
Tunjuk
Marga
Antegana
Pegubugan
Ngis
Sandan
Lembung
Beng
Manseke
Selamadeg
Kesiyut
Wanasari
Taman Kupu Kupu
(Bali Butterfly Park)
Gadungan
Timpak
Sarosi
Singing
Jelijih
Blubuk
Bluahan
Surabratan
Antosari
Megali
Rianggede
44
Lalang Linggah
Batuaji
Beach
Bajera
Srampingan
Pukuk
Sembunggede
Subamia-
baleagung
Calagi
Lod-
dalang
Bantas-
baleagung
Ambengan
Blayu
Meliling
Jadi
Mambang-
kadia
Tawakilang
Pura Alas
Kedaton
Antap
Soka
Cekik
Mandung
Tanjung Bulungdaya
Lumajang
Dukuhkanginan
Mambanggede
Santanbua
Samsam
Kamasan
4
Soka Beach
Bebali
Puri Agung
Tabanan
Tenebang
Bongan
Tista
Kukuh
Museum Subak
Mengwi
Klecung
Tanguntit
Sanggulan
Pang-
kungperabu
Jaketebe
Krambitan
Pangkung-
karung
Beraban
Blum-
bang
Papuan
Tibubiyu
Penarukan
Bonganpuseh
Kediri
Pasekan
Pasut Beach
Kelating
Pandak-
meranggi
Jempayah
Kalanganyar
Pejaten
Pura Desa/Puse
Kelatingdukuh
Sudimara
Pamesan
Nyitdah
Kelating Beach
Bengkel
Tangeb
Yeh Gangga
Belalang
Yeh Gangga Beach
Dauhjero
Kedungu
Beraban
Buduk
Tumbak-
bayuh
Dalung
Cemagi
Krobokan
Tanah Lot
Munggu
BADUNG
2
Pura Tanah Lot
Danginsema
3
Sangiangan
Babakan
Kangkang
Canggu
Pipitan
Kalibul
Mengening
Kulutulang
Seseh
Anyarbaleran
Pengem-
bungan
Banjar-
tengah
Tibu-
beneng
Kero-
bokan
Seseh Beach
Canggu Beach
Berawa
Malas
Batubelig
Pura Petitenget
Pengipian
Seminyak Beach
Samudera
Hindia
Legian Kaja
Teluk
Kuta
Legian
Legian Beach
2
Kuta
Kuta Beach
10
Abian Kuta
Ngurah Rai
Airport
Teluk
Jimbaran
Jimbaran
Jimbaran
Beach
Tanjung
Tegalwangi
Pura
Ulun
Siwi
Tanjung Balangan
Pantai Balangan
Tanjung Batupanggal
Teluk
Sait
Cengiling
Dreamland Beach
Pura Balangan
Gua
Peteng
(Pantai Padang Padang) Padang Padang Beach
Bangket
Simpangan
(Pantai Suluban) Suluban Beach
Labuan Sait
1
Tanjung Tanguma
Suluban
Bukit
12
Umpeng
Pura
Pererepan
Bakung
Pura Luhur Ulu Watu
Gunung Diana
182 m
Ulu Watu
Ungasan
6
Pecatu
125 m
Nyang Nyang
Beach
Pura
Masuka
A
B
C

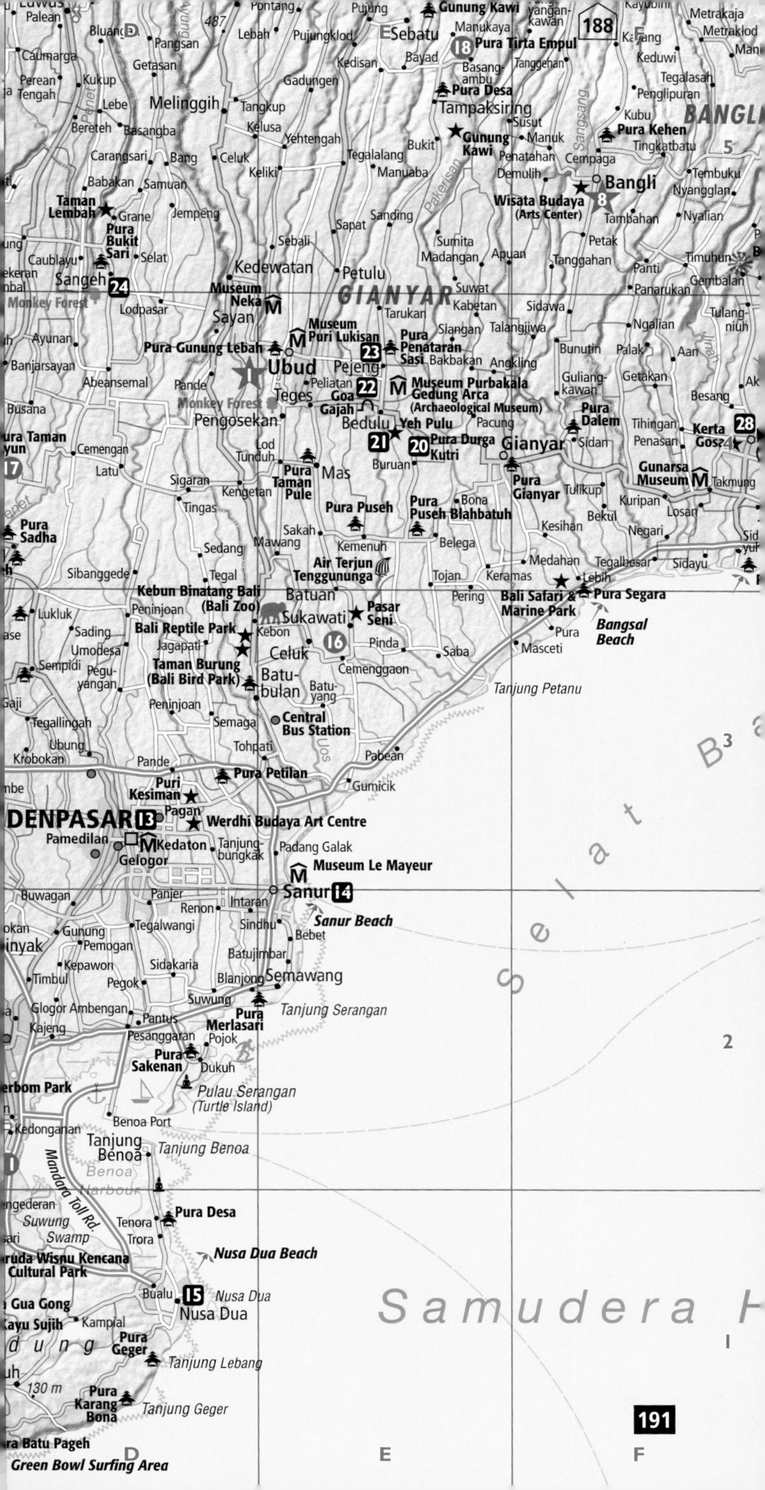

Palean
Bluang
D
Pangsan
487
Pontang
Lebah
Pujungklod
Pujung
E
Sebatu
Gunung Kawi
Manukaya
yangan-kawan
188
Kayubihi
Kajang
F
Metrakaja
Metraklod
Caumarga
Getasan
18
Pura Tirta Empul
Keduwi
Perean Tengah
Kukup
Gadungen
Kedisan
Bayad
Basang-ambu
Tanggehan
Tegalasah
Lebe
Melinggih
Tangkup
Pura Desa
Penglipuran
Bereteh
Basangba
Kelusa
Tampaksiring
Susut
Kubu
BANGLI
Yehtengah
Gunung Kawi
Manuk
Pura Kehen
Carangsari
Bang
Celuk
Tegalalang
Bukit
Penatahan
Cempaga
Tingkatbatu
5
Keliki
Manuaba
Demulih
Tembuku
Babakan
Samuan
Pakerisan
Bangli
Nyanglan
Taman Lembah
Grane
Jempeng
Sapat
Sanding
Wisata Budaya (Arts Center)
8
Tambahan
Nyalian
Pura Bukit Sari
Sebali
Sumita
Petak
Caublayu
Selat
Madangan
Apuan
Tanggahan
Timuhun
Sangeh
24
Kedewatan
Petulu
Panti
Gembalan
Monkey Forest
Museum Neka
GIANYAR
Suwat
Panarukan
Lodpasar
Sayan
Tarukan
Kabetan
Sidawa
Tulang-niuh
Ayunan
Museum Puri Lukisan
Pura Penataran Sasi
Siangan
Talangjiwa
Ngalian
Pura Gunung Lebah
23
Bunutin
Palak
Aan
Banjarsayan
Ubud
Pejeng
Bakbakan
Angkling
1
Peliatan
22
Museum Purbakala Gedung Arca
Guliang-kawan
Getakan
Abeansemal
Pande
Teges
Goa Gajah
(Archaeological Museum)
Besang
Busana
Monkey Forest
Pengosekan
Bedulu
Yeh Pulu
Pacung
Pura Dalem
Tihingan
Kerta Gosa
28
Cemengan
Lod Tunduh
21
20
Pura Durga Kutri
Gianyar
Sidan
Penasan
17
Latu
Mas
Buruan
Gunarsa Museum
Takmung
Sigaran
Kengetan
Pura Taman Pule
Pura Gianyar
Tulikup
Kuripan
Tingas
Pura Puseh
Pura Puseh Blahbatuh
Bona
Bekul
Losan
Pura Sadha
Sakah
Kesihan
Negari
Sedang
Mawang
Kemenuh
Belega
Medahan
Tegalbesar
Sidayu
Sibanggede
Tegal
Air Terjun Tenggunungan
Tojan
Keramas
Lebih
Kebun Binatang Bali (Bali Zoo)
Batuan
Pering
Bali Safari & Marine Park
Pura Segara
Lukluk
Peninjoan
Sukawati
Pasar Seni
Bangsal Beach
Sading
Bali Reptile Park
Kebon
Pura Masceti
Umodesa
Jagapati
Celuk
16
Pinda
Saba
Sempidi
Pegu-yangan
Taman Burung (Bali Bird Park)
Batu-bulan
Cemenggaon
Batu-yang
Tanjung Petanu
Peninjoan
Tegallingah
Semaga
Central Bus Station
Ubung
Tohpati
Uos
Krobokan
Pande
Pabean
B
3
Pura Petilan
Puri Kesiman
Gumicik
DENPASAR
13
Pagan
Werdhi Budaya Art Centre
t
Pamedilan
Kedaton
Tanjung-bungkak
Padang Galak
Gelogor
Museum Le Mayeur
a
Buwagan
Panjer
Sanur
14
Renon
Intaran
l
Gunung
Tegalwangi
Sindhu
Sanur Beach
Pemogan
Bebet
e
Kepawon
Sidakaria
Batujimbar
Timbul
Pegok
Blanjong
Semawang
S
Suwung
Glogor Ambengan
Pantus
Pura Merlasari
Tanjung Serangan
Kajeng
Pesanggaran
Pojok
2
Pura Sakenan
Dukuh
Pulau Serangan (Turtle Island)
Benoa Port
Kedonganan
Tanjung Benoa
Tanjung Benoa
Mandara Toll Rd.
Benoa Harbour
Suwung Swamp
Pura Desa
Tenora
Trora
Cultural Park
Nusa Dua Beach
Bualu
15
Nusa Dua
Nusa Dua
Samudera
Gua Gong
Kampial
Pura Geger
Tanjung Lebang
130 m
Pura Karang Bona
Tanjung Geger
Green Bowl Surfing Area
D
E
F

189
Royal Ponds
Tirtagangga
Klungkung (Semarapura)
KLUNGKUNG
Padang Bai
Candi Dasa
Teluk Amuk
Pura Goa Lawah
Goa Lawah (Bat Cavern)
Kusamba
Saltern
Pura Batu Klotok
Bukit Jambul
Pura Asmara
Bali Aga Village
Tenganan
Pura Silayukti
Balina Beach
Sengkidu Beach
Mendira Beach
Pasir Putih
Candi Dasa Beach
Padang Bai Beach
Nusa Kambing
Gili Tepekong
Gili Mimpang
Tanjung Sari
Tanjung Setra
Nusa Lembongan
Jungutbatu
Lembongan
Nusa Ceningan
Nusa Penida
Toyapakeh
Ped
Pura Dalem Penataran Ped
Sampalan
Goa Karangsari
Karangsari
Gunung Mundi 529 m
Tanjung Moling
Tanjung Bakung
Tanjung Biasmentik
Sebuluh
Klumpu
Batumadeg
Tanglad
826 m
a d u n g
Hindia

Index

Picture Credits

Getty Images: Matthew Wakem 6/7, Otto Stadler 18, Michele Falzone 23, Agung Parameswara 82, John Elk III 91, Jürgen Ritterbach 92, Michael Dean Morgan 100, Dallas Stribley 118, Ignacio Palacios 135, Brand X Pictures 138, Pandu Adnyana 139, joSon 140, Putu Sayoga 153, Wolfgang Pölzer 155, Peter Ptschelinzew 156, Nigel Killeen 166–168, Evgenia Bakanova 170, Russ Rohde 174

Glow Images: imagebroker 86/87, PhotoNonStop 143

huber-images: M. Bortoli 13, Brook Mitchell 20, Konstantin Trubavin 45, 46, Brook Mitchell 113, Bruno Cossa 131

laif: Frank Heuer 4, 8, hemis.fr/Stéphane Godin 10, Frank Heuer 16, 21, Andreas Hub 24, REA/Pierre Bessard 27, hemis.fr/Marc Dozier 29, 30, Frank Heuer 47, hemis.fr/Reinhard Dirscherl 48/49, Naftali Hilger 50, hemis.fr/Romain Cintract 55, hemis.fr/Franck Chaput 58, Frank Heuer 60, hemis.fr/Jean Du Boisberranger 61, hemis.fr/Camille Moirenc 62, hemis.fr/Franck Chaput 71, Redux/Patrick Love 73, Malte Jäger 76, 79, Redux/VWPics/Mikel Bilbao 90, hemis.fr/Franck Chaput 102, hemis.fr/Julien Garcia 104/105, Andreas Hub 114, Frank Heuer 133, hemis.fr/Franck Chaput 137, Frank Heuer 141, 142, hemis.fr/Franck Chaput 159, Bruno Morandi 160, Aurora/Konstantin Trubavin 161, Eva Häberle 169, Clemens Emmler 172

LOOK-foto: Rötting & Pollex 14, 15, Design Pics 51, Rötting & Pollex 74, Kay Maeritz 80, Rötting & Pollex 88, Rötting & Pollex 107, robertharding 108, Rötting & Pollex 110–112, age fotostock 128, 129, Rötting & Pollex 144, 145, Kay Maeritz 154

mauritius images: age/Charles O. Cecil 11, age/Michel Renaudeau 16/17, Alamy/Peter Eastland 17, Westend61/Peter Schickert 19, age/Christopher Leggett 25, Alamy/Peter Treanor 26, age/Colin Monteath 44, age/Chua Wee Boo 53, Westend61/Thomas Haupt 57, Westend61 70, John Warburton-Lee 75, Westend61/Konstantin Trubavin 77, Stefan Hefele 89, Westend61/Konstantin Trubavin 116, robertharding/G. & M. Therin-Weise 117, Pacific Stock/Dave Fleetham 120, imagebroker/Bernd Bieder 157

picture-alliance: robertharding/Luca Tettoni 119, Photoshot/BCI/Bruce Coleman 158

vario images: imagebroker 52, RHPL 83, imagebroker 84, AGF Creative 109

On the cover: Getty images/Martin Puddy (top, bottom), Getty Images (background)

1st Edition 2018

Worldwide Distribution: Marco Polo Travel Publishing Ltd
Pinewood, Chineham Business Park
Crockford Lane, Chineham
Basingstoke, Hampshire RG24 8AL, United Kingdom.

Authors: Michael Möbius
Translation: Robert Scott McInnes, Mödling
Editor: Margaret Howie, www.fullproof.co.za
Program supervisor: Birgit Borowski
Chief editor: Rainer Eisenschmid

Cartography: © MAIRDUMONT GmbH & Co. KG, Ostfildern
3D-illustrations: jangled nerves, Stuttgart

Printed in China

Despite all of our authors' thorough research, errors can creep in. The publishers do not accept any liability for this. Whether you want to praise us, alert us to errors or give us a personal tip – please don't hesitate to email or post to:

MARCO POLO Travel Publishing Ltd
Pinewood, Chineham Business Park
Crockford Lane, Chineham
Basingstoke, Hampshire RG24 8AL
United Kingdom
Email: sales@marcopolouk.com

10 REASONS
TO COME BACK AGAIN

1. You have to return to experience the more than **1,000 festivals and celebrations** held every year.
2. Bali's **volcanic landscapes** are among the most spectacular on earth.
3. The warmth and **friendly hospitality** on the Island of Smiles will keep you coming back.
4. You spent all your time exploring the temples and missed out on the **underwater world**.
5. You can never tire of the **culinary variety** of Indonesian-Balinese cuisine.
6. Your **nights in Kuta** were so long that the days were just too short.
7. **Bali's culture**, which permeates every aspect of daily life, is unique.
8. Bali's enchanting **rice terraces** are so lovely you'll want to see them more than once.
9. The deep **spirituality** of the Balinese never ceases to fascinate.
10. Bali is not just a resort island; it is a **dream destination**, beautiful enough to be experienced a second time.